CCCC Studies in Writing & Rhetoric

A Taste for Language

Literacy, Class, and English Studies

James Ray Watkins Jr.

Southern Illinois University Press
Carbondale

Printed in the United States of America

Publication partially funded by a subvention grant from the Conference on College Composition and Communication of the National Council of Teachers of English.

12 11 10 09 4 3 2 1

Frontispiece: James Ray Watkins Sr., circa 1944

Library of Congress Cataloging-in-Publication Data
Watkins, James Ray, 1958–
A taste for language : literacy, class, and English studies / James Ray Watkins Jr.
p. cm. — (CCCC studies in writing & rhetoric)
Includes bibliographical references and index.
ISBN-13: 978-0-8093-2931-1 (alk. paper)
ISBN-10: 0-8093-2931-X (alk. paper)
1. English philology—Study and teaching (Higher)—United States. 2. English language—Rhetoric—Study and teaching (Higher)—United States. I. Title.
PE68.U5W37 2009
428.0071'173—dc22 2009011132

Printed on recycled paper.
The paper used in this publication meets the minimum requirements of American National Standard for Information Sciences—Permanence of Paper for Printed Library Materials, ANSI Z39.48-1992.

This text is dedicated to the life and memory of my father, James Ray Watkins Sr.

I have known the inexorable sadness of pencils,
Neat in their boxes, dolor of pad and paper-weight,
All the misery of manila folders and mucilage,
Desolation in immaculate public places,
Lonely reception room, lavatory, switchboard . . .

—Theodore Roethke, "Dolor"

CONTENTS

Acknowledgments

I would like to thank Professor Andrew Cooper, who told me more than fifteen years ago that I should do what I felt I had to do, and when and if I was ever ready to return to the life of an academic, he would help. Without Dr. Cooper, this book may not have ever happened. Dr. Harry Cleaver started me on this road, a long time ago, and Dr. Linda Ferreira-Buckley listened and talked to me at more than one key moment. Professors Slatin, Syverson, Stott, Kimball, and Barrish had the unenviable task of shepherding what must have seemed an outlandish proposition at its earliest stages. Each has kept me honest, and each taught me something of the discipline that must guide ambition if it is to be fruitful. I must thank my academic, union, and personal friends and colleagues, in no particular order. Among my friends and colleagues from Texas, I include Lisa Sue Garbus, Lupe Gomez, Anne Marsella, Kazel Morgan, Lynn McCray, Albert Rouzie, and Lynn Rudloff. My friends and colleagues in Philadelphia include Gretel Pillar, Eli Goldblatt, Lori Salem, Jill Swavely, Steve Parks, Susan Wells, Hank Barrenger, and Amy Birge; those in Illinois, Tim Engles and Suk Ja Kang Engles, Angela Vietto, Lauren Smith, and Carol Jean Dudley. Without the advice and support of these friends, I might well have simply given up. I would like to thank my mother, Trista Klibert Watkins; my sisters, Cynthia, Lisa, and Jill, and their husbands, Donald Lack, James Gram, and Cliff Ainsworth; and my nieces and nephews, Megan and Lindsay Lack, Cynthia Reine, Nicholas and Stephanie Gram, and Aaron and Brianna Rae Ainsworth. I owe a great deal to Robert Brooke, who first saw something valuable in my manuscript, and to John Brereton and Nancy Welch, who provided insightful reviews. Also, I'd like to thank Joseph Harris for his always productive editing suggestions. Neil Ching's indexing services were invaluable. I have to mention my dog, too, Lady Bear. Finally, I owe more than I can say to Elise Hempel and her daughter, Neenah Rafiqi.

A TASTE FOR LANGUAGE

Introduction: Written English, English Studies, and the Analysis of Class

> Imagine a society entirely absorbed in its own historicity. It would be incapable of producing historians. Living entirely under the sign of the future, it would satisfy itself with automatic self-recording processes and auto-inventory machines, postponing indefinitely the task of understanding itself. By contrast, our society—torn from its memory by the scale of the transformations but all the more obsessed with understanding itself historically—is forced to give an increasingly central role to the operations that take place within the historian. The historian is one who prevents history from becoming merely history.
>
> —Pierre Nora, "Between Memory and History: Les Lieux de Memoire"

EDUCATION AND THE AMERICAN DREAM

THIS IS A BOOK about the American dream as it has become embodied in the university in general and in the English department in particular. It is, admittedly, a utopian story, a narrative of the highest and perhaps most impossible desires of human culture. Yet I hope it is also a very practical book about the history of English studies, a vision of where I believe we ought to go, and at least the start of a field guide to how we might get there. To paraphrase Pierre Nora's "Between Memory and History," it's about English studies, but it's also about the English studies professional.

This is also a book about my father and me and about the ways that his life has shaped my own academic and linguistic interests. The version of the American dream we have collaboratively achieved over two generations, in other words, is deeply rooted in the historical purposes embodied by the study of language and literature at the university level. Traditionally, the emblematic figure of English studies has been the heroic literary academic struggling to convince a plebian culture that his or her work is vital to its future. That figure, however absurd it may seem when phrased so bluntly, remains deeply embedded in the academic culture of our field. It is, arguably, a story that has outlived its usefulness. In this sense, English studies is in profound crisis.

In order to deflate the romance of the literary academic, we have to begin to understand its origins and purposes. In doing so, we can start to rethink the place of English studies—indeed, of education—in American society. In my study, I want to offer a counter-myth: the student who comes to college to get what he or she needs in order to live a life more prosperous than his or her parents'. In this counter-narrative, the student leaves college with a transformed notion of affluence and success and with ideas about knowledge, the self, and the world that have a particular, substantive relationship to language and to writing. In creating this counter-narrative, I tell the story of my father's transformation from the son of a tenant farmer to an accountant, from poverty in rural Mississippi to relative affluence in suburban Texas. The keys to this transformation, I argue, are the GI Bill and a university education. My father also raised a son who became a professor in an English department, and part of this story will be to try to understand how that first education, in some sense, shaped the second.

This too, then, is a book about socioeconomic class, and so it must necessarily confront what writer/critic bell hooks has called the silence that surrounds class in American society, particularly in the classroom:

> Nowhere is there a more intense silence about the reality of class differences than in educational settings. . . . From grade school on, we are all encouraged to cross the threshold of the classroom believing that we are entering a democratic space—a free zone where the desire to study and learn makes us all equal. . . . [T]he underlying assumption is that we are all

> equally committed to . . . moving up the ladder to the top. And even though many of us will not make it to the top, the unspoken assumption is that we will land somewhere in the middle, between top and bottom. (177)

This "unspoken assumption" about class and education—that through college all have at least a chance of economic and social betterment and that material privilege is earned rather than inherited—extends to the very definition of class and to what we mean when we say "middle." If hooks's argument is correct, and most of us who are educated do end up "between top and bottom," then as a culture we have a pressing need to understand more fully what it means to be middle-class. We need a way to speak of class that encompasses money as well as culture, and we need to ask whether or not the status so many of our parents sought is in fact at all desirable in a democratic society.

The American dream is a collective story of needs and wishes beyond any one person's requirements or hopes. This, then, is necessarily a book about class, and class mobility, and education, but it rejects visions of the American dream that make success sound easy or complete or individualistic. In that sense, this is also a dystopian tale of desire gone horribly wrong. Indeed, I argue that our shared image of education in general and of English studies in particular has become radically small-minded and narrow, too limited in what we want for ourselves, our society, and our students. That lack of vision and a concurrent failure of will are our greatest losses. English studies once represented a concerted effort to create a new kind of affluent society through a direct confrontation with the injustices of socioeconomic class and the ideologies of positivism; all too often it now seems a weak link in an education system reduced to the meager aims of vocation and professional self-preservation.

English studies, in short, has always been about class and class mobility. My argument, however, is that the traditional form of this historical project has lost its usefulness and vitality. What English studies needs, then, is a new sense of class and of its place within the democratic desire for class mobility. My book has a two-part structure that accurately reflects, I hope, what I consider to be the bifurcated needs of contemporary English studies. The first three chapters focus on a revisionist history of our field, conceptualized in terms of socioeconomic class in general and of Pierre Bourdieu's formulations of cultural capital in particular. The second half of the book, beginning with a reconsideration of the debates over English studies at midcentury, attempts to articulate a progressive vision of the future. Our agenda, I argue, must be both pedagogical and professional, encompassing a defense of our form of employment as well as a new definition of the cultural capital we accumulate and then distribute more widely through our institutions. Our revised sense of class, in other words, has to include an understanding of our own socioeconomic status as well as a set of educational ideals. I want to begin, then, with an extended discussion of Bourdieu's analysis of class in the context of a university-level education in English language and literature.

PIERRE BOURDIEU: ETHOS AND AESTHETICS AS CULTURAL CAPITAL

English studies, as many have said, can be usefully conceived as being about the study of writing, yet such a reconceptualization often rests too easily on a set of unexamined assumptions about language, curricular sequence, and development, as if the writing taught in first-year courses was merely a simpler, less sophisticated prototype for that of the literary seminar, and the composition student was always already destined to become a poet or a professor. The hierarchy embodied in that progression lies at the heart of our current professional stalemate. In rethinking English studies, in other words, we cannot ignore the symbolic and material gulf that separates the memo from the poem, the first-year writer from the artist, and the adjunct from the tenured, to cite only the most obvious of examples.

English studies, in short, embraces two different traditions of writing, that of literary studies and that of rhetoric and composition, each with distinct, if not contradictory, intellectual and pedagogical pedigrees. Far from a simple matter of curriculum, or even of remedial necessity, these differing histories reflect contrasting epistemologies, what sociologist Bourdieu has called the popular ethos and the formalist aesthetic (*Distinction* 5). On the one hand, the history of rhetoric and composition, viewed in this light, is rooted in a notion of writing that sees language as a transparent medium for thought, a means to the larger social good of effective and honest communication. In contrast, literary studies is founded on an aesthetic discourse that values formal experimentation and that defines language as a translucent medium for creative expression and an end in itself.

Remaking English studies means, therefore, rethinking the historical and theoretical meaning of the relationship between ethos and aesthetics, a dynamic that drives English studies in all of its manifestations, from creative to professional writing, linguistics to the more contemporary interest in so-called creative nonfiction and new media. These epistemologies have differing efficacies in the world, even if we recognize that in practice we move more or less freely between the two. In fact, that ability to shift from a framework of ethos to one of aesthetics, a fluency in conceptual or epistemological code-switching, succinctly defines the cultural capital of English studies, in terms of its portfolio of abilities and knowledge as accumulated by the professors and of the horizon of sensibility toward which we wish to move our pupils and so our culture. Taken together, these epistemologies of ethos and aesthetics constitute what Bourdieu describes (speaking of the "habitus" more generally) as a "matrix of perceptions, appreciations, and actions" that "makes possible the achievement of infinitely diversified tasks" in language (*Outline* 83). This matrix, if read strictly as embodied in our traditional curriculum, might seem simplistic, as if ethos and aesthetics were quarantined off into separate realms and linguistic taste was bound by academic structure. Nothing could be farther from the truth.

In composition classes, students can be held to quite high formal and aesthetic standards; in literary assignments, they can be asked to adhere to the strictest ethos of communication. In a creative writing class, students may focus solely on the production of writing according to the strictures of the formalist aesthetic; a literature class might be focused on learning to decode a formalist aesthetic while producing texts more accurately described as governed by a popular ethos.

At the same time, success for English department professors in the modern U.S. education system has always meant that they both understand and value literary language, particularly but not solely in their research work, as well as communicate effectively, particularly but not solely in their service and teaching activities. Nonetheless, what has remained consistently distorted, and what I hope this book might help to restore, is our understanding of the relationship between ethos and aesthetics. Most important, English studies as it is now institutionalized places aesthetics over ethos, contending through its labor practices and institutional rewards as well as through its teaching that aesthetics is more important, more intellectually substantive, than ethos. This hierarchy has had myriad effects, material as well as symbolic.

At one level, the hierarchy in English studies shapes employment practices in English departments, ensuring that traditionally, as has been often noted, specialists in ethos are less well compensated for their efforts, have less secure institutional positions, and, as in too much of U.S. culture, are more often female. Ideologically, the devaluing of ethos in English studies complements the emergence of what has been called the neoliberal university and its casualization of academic labor, a process equally dependent on literary studies' inability to conceptualize a historically relevant narrative of legitimacy. If ethos is as intellectually slight as traditional academic culture has always implied, it can be taught by adjuncts. In the culture at large, in other words, ethos and aesthetics have come to be valued quite differently than in English studies, and for quite different reasons. In contemporary culture, ethos resonates with a kind of practical vocational efficacy.

Historically and institutionally, the practices of rhetoric and composition were founded in a rationalization of ethos read against the complexities of aesthetics, and so in a misrepresentation of the social import of taste. Ethos represented training and skill; aesthetics, knowledge and talent. Yet, as I hope to show, ethos, too, is a matter of sensibility as well as of knowledge. The contemporary field of rhetoric and composition has its origins in a rejection of this simple formulation of linguistic ethos, but the effects of this ethos cannot be expunged without a fundamental institutional change that has yet to happen.

Bourdieu's sociology of class suggests that we understand college-level education in the English language as an attempt to make the linguistic cultural capital of the student more similar to the linguistic cultural capital of the teacher, an intimate transmission not simply of knowledge but of sensibility. That is, pedagogy can be understood as one dimension of a process through which we internalize tastes in language, itself an aspect of what Bourdieu terms the inculcation of a habitus. The inculcation of taste, and the creation of a habitus, Bourdieu contends, happens in the family as well as in school and in society at large; like economic capital, it is less a singular object, like a commodity, than an ongoing process of accumulation. The cultural capital of English studies, in other words, isn't analogous to money but to an investment portfolio. What's more, I believe that one of the central disappointments of English studies thus far is its ongoing blindness about the workings of its own cultural capital, a blindness matched only by the insights it has gained into the cultural life outside its often insular walls.

Taking concepts drawn from Bourdieu's sociology of socioeconomic class as my starting point, I argue that English studies ought to be redefined in terms of how it shapes and is shaped by linguistic taste as a form of cultural capital. Understanding English studies as a system of cultural capital, in other words, allows us to understand our field in a thoroughly historical way, distinct but not separate from the capitalist economy as a whole. Far from rejecting the education of taste as an elitist enterprise, I contend that an education in taste represents a crucial, indeed inescapable, part of the ongoing struggle for social justice in our society, a struggle too often thought of as merely a redistribution of economic capital. In short, class cannot be reduced to finances, and the class mobility traditionally sought through education is more than a struggle for a better job.

The historical purpose of English studies has always been to create in students a transformative passion for language, an education that would change not just students but society. This progressive ideology is the now obscured heart of the historical project of the U.S. middle class. Behind English studies lies a set of assumptions about language, and behind those, a set of desires for a world in which sheer material need has lost its dominating power. The "middle" that hooks identifies, too often maligned as narrowly materialistic, is in fact an image of a society without the twin malignancies of great wealth and horrible poverty. Defining our history in terms of cultural capital and taste allows us to reconnect to core democratic values and to forge links among the aims and goals of the classroom, our own desires for justice in the workplace and in the world, the cultural capital of students as well as professors, and the economic and social system that everywhere influences what we do and think. English studies is, in this view, a singular mission of equally singular complexity, and its future depends on our ability to return coherence and vision to our curriculum.

THE IMBROGLIOS OF EDUCATION AND CLASS

Any understanding of education—much less an education in language—necessarily attests to what Bruno Latour has called the contemporary "imbroglios" of knowledge. That is, an education is a hybrid phenomenon in which "all of culture and all of nature get churned up" (6). "Press the most innocent aerosol button," Latour writes, "and you'll be heading for the Antarctic, and from there to the University of California at Irvine, the mountain ranges of Lyon, the chemistry of inert gasses, and then maybe to the United Nations" (6). The "hole in the ozone layer," in other words, cannot be accounted for by or through adherence to disciplinary and academic divisions and boundaries; it is about physics as much as sociology, economics as much as psychology.

Yet Latour argues that, when faced with this complexity, researchers too often seem most interested in what might be called a misplaced disciplinary loyalty: "Analysts, thinkers, journalists and decision-makers will slice the delicate network into tidy compartments where you will find only science, only economy, only social phenomena, only local news. . . . [T]his fragile thread will be broken into as many segments as there are pure disciplines" (7). Similarly, an investigation into an education is an exploration of a process made up of students, textbooks, teachers, institutions, and families; it is as economic as it is cognitive, as personal as it is social. An education, too, is a hybrid in which "all of culture and all of nature get churned up" and that therefore cannot be coherently accounted for by remaining solely within the "tidy compartments" of academic disciplines. Yet, as I hope will become clear, much current research into university-level English language and literature too often seems attenuated in this way, reducing an education such as my father's into merely national culture, or uncomplicated economics, or even solely a matter of language. As hooks might say, the cost of maintaining these compartments has become prohibitively expensive, a quietude that I would argue we can no longer afford.

What interests me here as a son, a researcher, and a teacher is precisely the hybridism of my father's education, the "fragile thread" intertwining object and subject, individual and institution, time and space. We are "hybrids ourselves," Latour writes, and as such ought to be interested in investigative pathways rather than in disciplines: "We have chosen to follow these imbroglios wherever they may take us. To shuttle back and forth we rely on the notion of translation, or network. More subtle than the notion of system, more historical than the notion of structure, more empirical than the notion of complexity, the idea of network is the Ariadne's thread of these interwoven stories" (7). In Latour's terms, then, my query cannot aspire to an exhaustive analysis of the historical and social phenomena relevant to my father's education. In lieu of neat finality, I offer the "interwoven stories" of biography, socioeconomic class, college courses, and institutional structures represented by my father's undergraduate degree. I cannot rely on interviews, either, since my father died long before I began the course of study that initiated this project. Instead, I must draw on memory and social history, as much as on transcripts and textbooks. I offer little empirical proof, in other words, that my father's case is typical of the men of his generation or of their education, even if, at certain moments, it seems quite clear that he shared ideas and experiences common to his time and place. Instead, a biographical and historical approach will allow me to go into specific detail and so take into account more sorts of evidence than a narrowly focused statistical or sociological study would allow.

The distinctive form of my father's literacy, rooted in his story and in the social and economic forces of his time and shaped in particular by his university education, presents a unique challenge in reconstructing an otherwise unnoted history. As Richard Rodriguez has said of his own autobiographical work, "Some people have told me how wonderful it is that I am the first in the family to write a book. I stand on the edge of a long silence. But I do not give voice to my parents by writing about their lives. I distinguish myself from them by writing about the life we once shared" (3). Like Rodriguez's work, this study "stand[s] on the edge of a long silence," on an almost uncanny lack of cultural discussion and reflection about class, and on a family history whose only formal representations are official records and texts. The writing my father produced (student papers in college and memos throughout his professional life) and the kind of man he was—a subject I return to periodically—make textual and archival evidence all too rare. Likewise, the specific forms of his classroom instruction, including the syllabi and even the names of his instructors, are largely lost, documentation presumably only rarely thought worthy of preservation.

My father was able to attend college despite financial and social difficulties; his service in the army, among other things, allowed him to escape what Rodriguez terms the "real work" of physical labor. One of the premises of this study, however, is that private silences can and do persist. As Rodriguez writes: "Once upon a time I was a 'socially disadvantaged' child. An enchantedly happy child. Mine was a childhood of intense family closeness. And extreme public alienation. Thirty years later I write this book as a middle-class American man. Assimilated" (3). Rodriguez offers us the story of a nominally complete, if painful, assimilation, the romance of his transformation from a working-class child to an upper-middle-class writer. His text, he contends, breaks the long silence of a hard-working but uneducated family, and he writes "surrounded by volumes of

Montaigne and Shakespeare and Lawrence. They are mine now" (5). In contrast, my own writing, both autobiographical and biographical, must attempt to explore the Ariadne's thread of a heretofore less public, more inarticulate sensibility, one in which "Montaigne and Shakespeare and Lawrence" had little place. Here, perhaps, my father's story begins to move outside of the territory usually covered in the American success story.

Necessarily, then, my study begins in what might be seen as an inherently ambiguous effort to authenticate a largely undocumented life. In this sense, my work represents my own imaginative effort to speak for and to my father, to break the long silence of his life and his literacy, to seek out the boundaries between the facts I can collect and the events I can only surmise. A fundamental premise of this study is that what Latour calls a purification process can only forestall the sorts of subtly detailed examinations of education that are needed in the midst of the fundamental changes now underway at universities and English departments across the United States. Our contemporary predicaments—economic restructuring, budget cuts and unprecedented deficits, war and terror and what seems a revitalized, violent U.S. imperialism—surely obligate the clearest understanding of the history and meaning of the profession of English studies and its place in our culture. More locally, the ongoing introduction of computer technology into the college classroom, the changing status of rhetoric and composition as well as of literature itself, and the rise in contingent employment, to cite only the most obvious examples, together exemplify a remarkable and potentially radical transformation of university instruction in English.

Arguably, the English studies that educated both my father and me is steadily unraveling, in danger of being rewoven into an institution neither of us would or could support. In such an environment, I would contend, the most elementary questions about literacy, language, literature, education, and class—the questions that shaped my father's goals for himself as well as for his children—have once again become imperative. What purposes does an education in English language and literature serve in the lives of the educated in a class society? What are the sources and effects of the division between practical and existential or personally transformative pedagogies? If many students, unlike Rodriguez, do not emerge from the classroom as professional writers and intellectuals, what do they take away from their college classes in English? Is English wholly irrelevant in this new century?

1

My Father's Education

> Unsightly and slovenly papers on the whole are like people with dirty necks and uncombed hair. No person of good taste and intelligence would appear in public without having given attention to his appearance. But a person's writing is certainly as important as his outward appearance. It is a part of him, is an ambassador which appears for him when he is absent: it should therefore be in appearance what the writer would like to be in appearance himself.
>
> —Gerald D. Sanders, Hoover H. Jordan, Robert M. Limpus, and Wallace H. Magoon, *Unified English Composition*

HOUSECLEANING

IN THE FALL OF 1998, two of my three sisters and I spent several long weekends helping my mother, then sixty-eight, clean out the house in Houston, Texas, where she had lived for the previous thirty-five years. All of us agreed that the place was too big for an older woman living alone and that she should sell her home. My mother, naturally, had little desire to leave the house where she had raised four children and lived with her husband until his death. A few months earlier, however, she had fallen, and while she was not hurt, the experience had been a revelation about growing old without having anyone else nearby. Eventually, we hoped, my sister Cynthia and her husband, Don, would build a widow's wing for her in their planned new house in Sulphur, Louisiana. Mom could be close to two of her seven grandchildren, Megan and Lindsey, and, away from the crowded highways of Houston, she might preserve her independence under her eldest daughter's watchful eye.

My mother had accumulated a remarkable collection: furniture, clothes, photographs, Christmas decorations, magazines and catalogs, dishes, pots and pans, and financial records. The emptier the house had gotten over the years, it seemed, the harder my mother had worked to fill it. Some things one or the other of the siblings wanted to keep, but much of what she had acquired we packed up in cardboard boxes and sent off to the Salvation Army. The more useful items could be sold at a garage sale. My youngest sister, Jill, was in charge of that side of the enterprise. Piles of mortgage payments, bank statements, warranties, and receipts were sorted; we saved what Mom felt she needed and threw the rest out, filling plastic bag after plastic bag.

My father had died more than sixteen years earlier and had left little behind; after some effort, my mother had finally gotten rid of the rest of his clothes and his few possessions. We kept only what seemed to best capture our memories of him: several pipes and the smoking paraphernalia that he loved, his driver's license, a pair of glasses, a small number of papers related to his work as a CPA, his college diploma, a small bone-handled pocketknife. On a bookshelf alongside the *National Geographic* magazines and the *Reader's Digests*, we found a handful of his college textbooks, including Jane Austen's *Pride and Prejudice.* Most important for my purposes here, we found his college composition textbook, *Unified English Composition.* F. S. Crofts first published the book, written collaboratively by Gerald D. Sanders, Hoover H. Jordan, Robert M. Limpus, and Wallace H. Magoon of the Michigan State Normal College, in 1942. My father's copy, from 1946, was the eleventh printing.

Carefully cradling the old textbook in her hands, my mother recalled that Dad had had quite a bit of trouble in the first few years of college. His teachers, she explained, felt that he needed to correct what they called a stutter; it was a little strange, she had thought even then, because his speech had seemed fine to her. Maybe he was simply nervous speaking in front of his class and needed extra help with a skill that anyone in business would surely need. The aims of college instructors, she hinted, were more than a little mysterious to them. Neither had much if any experience with such people.

My mother also remembered that when my father was struggling with his literature classes, she would help by reading the stories or poems aloud to him. Language—or, more specifically, accent or dialect—was a tiresome problem in the early years of their marriage and during my father's time at Louisiana State University (LSU). My mother was born and raised just north of New Orleans in the French-speaking community of Vacherie, and she was self-conscious about her heavy Cajun accent. She recalls changing her own way of speaking to more closely approximate what seemed to her to be the urban style of the women she met working at the capital building in Baton Rouge.

My research—and perhaps common sense, given the low status of composition in this period—suggests that universities of the 1940s rarely preserved materials from freshman composition. Thus far, I have not turned up any records of the materials or instructors at LSU who guided my father through what must have been the difficult passage of his first college year. Our search of the many files and papers hidden away in file folders and closets in my mother's house did not turn up a single example of the written assignments he surely completed to receive his degree. As an older adult, he may have found his early efforts at composition and literary exposition embarrassing, or, as my mother suspects, it could be that he simply discarded them in our move from Louisiana to Texas in the early 1960s. In any case, the paucity of records seems to me emblematic of the place of reading and writing in his life.

Nevertheless, some documents representative of the writing my father did as a professional did survive. These include a handwritten draft of his résumé, from the mid-1970s, and a series of job descriptions he was asked to produce at around the same time; a letter to the Veterans Administration requesting that his date of birth be officially corrected; a letter to the Post Exchange in Fort Dix, New Jersey, regarding a misplaced insurance policy; and a short memo entitled "Rates and Research Major Activities 1972." In addition, there are copies of his entry in *Who's Who in the Southwest* and two newspaper articles from the *Houston Chronicle* (again, from the early 1970s). Almost all of the documents that my father deemed important enough to keep relate in some way to his long struggle to receive adequate financial compensation for his position in the city government. Also among his records were a copy of job listings posted in the *Newsletter of the Texas Association of CPAs* (a position in North Carolina is underlined in pencil); materials from the local chapter of the American Association of State, County and Municipal Employees; and a memo from his superiors denying him reimbursement for the extensive driving expenses his position often required. He considered relocation, my mother tells me, but rejected the idea as too disruptive to his family.

Taken together, these documents and my father's textbook, *Unified English Composition*, offer an intriguing glimpse into university-level English education and its historical relationship to socioeconomic class and literacy. Like many other young men of the time, my father entered the army at age sixteen, claiming to be two years older and a high school graduate. In many senses, his future was settled by the circumstances of his birth. He should have stayed poor or working-class. Yet, in an accident of culture rooted in the violence of war, he was able to leave Mississippi, attend college, and become a professional. What's more, as an accountant he became what Deborah Brandt has recently called a knowledge worker, earning his living "by generating and leveraging knowledge" ("Writing" 166). As Brandt emphasizes, "The knowledge economy is heavily associated with brain power, creativity, and other so-called human capital" (167). How did my father—who quit school in the fourth grade and went to college after his military service—learn the meaning of writing as a cultural practice?

At a minimum, through his college education my father acquired the technical knowledge he needed to leave his working-class background behind, at least in a formal sense, and to function effectively in a middle-class professional setting. By the time he wrote the letters and memos discussed in this chapter, he was capable of producing texts free of grammatical and syntactical error. In this sense, these skills are a form of cultural capital that he had successfully invested and that paid economic and social dividends. My father never worked in what Brandt terms a writing-intensive profession, but central to the class transformation embodied in his education was the opportunity to earn his living intellectually rather than physically. Yet, as Pierre Bourdieu's research reminds us, class is also a matter of taste, an internalized sense of what is good or bad, beautiful or ugly, appropriate or inappropriate. Alongside our understanding of the linguistic skills my father acquired in college, we must ask another set of questions: What were the primary factors that shaped my father's taste in language? How can we define "appropriateness" in language in the American professional context? How does a student learn what is and is not acceptable in writing?

WRITING AS CULTURAL CAPITAL

In the first four chapters of this book, I explore the traditional cultural capital of English studies in a variety of ways, in hopes of sketching out at least the broad outlines of a revisionist and materialist history of language study at the university level in the United States. As I hope will become clear, the study of the written language in particular lies at the heart of the historical mission of the higher education system throughout the second and third quarters of the twentieth century. The reproduction and distribution of the linguistic cultural capital disseminated through this system, in turn, is rooted in a complex rhetoric of objectivity, professionalism, and merit. Arguably, this cultural capital—or, rather, these forms of cultural capital—played a key role in the economic and cultural successes of the middle class, particularly in the third quarter of the twentieth century. In the final two chapters of the book, then, I return to the present, to investigate how this revised historical understanding can illuminate contemporary developments in English studies.

As a start to this exploration, I would like to sketch out here the general shape of the pedagogical and ideological networks linking my father's college curriculum to his composition textbook and then to his professional writing. All of these artifacts can be read in terms of the larger economic and sociological systems in which my father led his life. In a powerful sense, his ability to move from a working-class and poor childhood to professional employment and the middle class was overdetermined by the historical circumstances in which he found himself. In another sense, of course, this transformation of sense and sensibility was a fragile, contingent bit of luck, dependent on impossible-to-duplicate events and choices.

In contrast to the commonly held view that literary studies dominated the college curriculum in the mid-twentieth century, I offer a more complex set of dynamic relationships between composition and literary courses, one that reflects the democratic ideals of class mobility that underlay U.S. higher education in this period. I begin this examination through an analysis of my father's life and education in terms of what Brandt has called the accumulation of literacy. Relying on Brandt as a starting point, I then move into a close reading of the pedagogical purposes embodied in the distribution of courses represented in my father's college transcript. The allocation of English language courses, I argue, is a clear echo of the goals of education as a methodology of class mobility. Instrumental language, moreover, played a central role in the way a liberal system approached the education of middle-class professionals.

In the next two sections, I provide a close reading of my father's textbook, *Unified English Composition*, focusing on the rhetorics of professional objectivity and merit that support its descriptions of language in general and of writing in particular. Objectivity, I contend, provided an ideological and ethical rationale for writing, while the rhetoric of merit emphasized that the cultural capital of composition had to be earned through hard work rather than inherited through family connections. I then briefly touch on the place of aesthetics in the textbook, an orientation that reflects my father's transcript in significant ways. In the fourth section, I show how these rhetorics of objectivity and merit were reflected in the ideological and ethical assumptions that underlie the reports my father wrote as an accountant for the city of Houston.

Finally, I conclude this chapter with a discussion of the silence—or silences—that characterize discussions of class in the United States, focusing particular attention on the relationships among class, literacy, and education in my father's aspirations and on his desires for his children. Among the most important of these silences, I contend, is our lack of an ongoing conversation about English studies as a system through which certain forms of cultural capital are shaped and distributed. I am particularly interested in how class mobility can be understood as a multigenerational project achieved over the course of two generations. My father went to school for utilitarian reasons, but the very success of those practical goals helped to create a wider, less pragmatic set of desires and choices for his children. In a sense, then, this chapter ends where it began, asking what it meant and might mean to be a literate member of the middle class.

LITERACY AND ACCUMULATION

What does literacy mean in the context of a college degree? First, in Brandt's useful term, literacy is "accumulated" rather than simply "acquired" ("Accumulating" 650). It occurs, Brandt writes, in the "often conflicted contexts of literacy" that a student inhabits (666). Literacy and, by extension, education, in other words, is not a singular skill or knowledge, acquired once and for all, but a series of interrelated, more or less successful learning experiences occurring over stretches of time and space and rooted in the specifics of both individual biography and social history. Put simply, my father learned to read and write in different sorts of institutions and situations over the course of his life, and this schooling had purposes and effects that were at times contradictory. It would be impossible, of course, to separate out in a specific way the educational sources of his attitudes about education and literacy from the myriad of more general possible causes. These ideas were certainly a part of the larger culture at the time; many if not most men of my father's generation surely had similar ideas, and the historical importance of literacy in the culture of the United States since the colonial period has been extensively explored.

It is possible, however, following Brandt, to outline the sequence of accumulations that occurred in my father's life, given the educational institutions he encountered and his social and economic background. The rural elementary school, for example, that he attended in Sumrall, Mississippi, in the 1930s could not have encouraged the same ideas about reading and writing as did the university he attended in urban Baton Rouge in the late 1940s. As Brandt puts it, somewhat dismissively, in the early years of the twentieth century, literacy was "shifting from the cultivated talk of the well-bred to the efficient professional prose of the technocrat" ("Accumulating" 659). Before my father went to college, the United States would endure the Great Depression and World War II. In his elementary classroom, he cultivated the basics of literacy and learned something of the importance of reading and writing, but the idea of a college education was a remote possibility. In fact, family circumstances helped to ensure that my father's primary-school education ended after the fourth grade.

It was only the intervention of the war, where he served as a tank commander in Europe from February 1942 to October 1945, and the GI Bill that made college an authentic possibility for men of my father's socioeconomic status. However limited, this biographical sketch does suggest some of the ways that the gaps and inconsistencies in his education would have made reading and writing troublesome for my father, not easily employed outside of more or less practical tasks. What's more, if his education in a rural school first helped to make him literate, his university experiences would later show him, in a very personal way, the importance of this early experience in reading and writing. College was difficult, he once told me, because when he began he had not been in a classroom since he was a young child; like many World War II veterans, he had to earn a high-school equivalency degree at a night school before his first year in the university. The military likely required little of him in terms of education beyond the basic knowledge he brought with him. Tank commanders, it was thought, while trained in a variety of skills, did not need much classroom experience to succeed (Palmer, Wiley, and Keast, *Army Ground Forces* 246–47).

Given this background, my father assuredly entered the college classroom motivated by some notion of the importance of education as a potential means to a better job and by an awareness of the limits and challenges his situation—past and present—had imposed. He brought with him the literacy he had accumulated, starting in his elementary school, and perhaps a sense of discipline and hierarchy from the military, but he had little concrete knowledge of higher education. No one in his immediate family had attended school much beyond the middle- or high-school level; his family, my mother tells me, saw college as a kind of indulgence and thought that any young man could better spend his time earning a living. Before he entered LSU, then, it is likely that my father had only the roughest approximation of what a university education might entail.

Brandt's ideas and the economic and historical setting of my father's life can help explicate in a general way my father's personal reading and writing habits, the choices he made in his education, and his goals for my own. Certainly, my father was predisposed toward the vocational values of English studies and so was perhaps less likely to aspire to what is often termed the liberal arts goal of "research for its own sake." Yet these ideas can say little about the meaning of the idea that an education could be a route to the kind of personal transformation implicit in his injunctions to me and my sisters. At LSU, he was certainly educated into a profession and into the norms of language associated with it, but just as certainly, I would argue, he brought out of that experience ideas and purposes that he felt were more appropriate for someone with an altogether different background from his own. My father left college with more than professional skills; he graduated with a larger sense of the purposes of education that made it imperative for his children as well. Again, for my father, entering the middle class meant more than a new job; if education was a practical matter when he entered college, by the time he graduated from LSU, it had become much more.

Alongside the "technocratic literacy" of his college curriculum, of course, were the seemingly less pragmatic goals of the liberal arts, nominally represented by courses in literature. His curriculum, in other words, precisely reflected the tension between skill and sensibility, ethos and aesthetics, that underlay his movement from working poor to soldier to educated professional. Still, my father's utilitarian educational aims were largely consistent with the overall distribution of courses in his undergraduate curriculum. He initially wanted to study law, my mother reports, but the GI Bill would not pay for an advanced program; he settled on what was then called a commerce degree. He attended LSU from September 1947 until the summer of 1950 and took forty-two classes over the course of six long and three summer semesters. His classes can be divided into three groups: first, courses specifically related to his major; second, a group of survey courses in various fields; and third, a cluster of courses related to English-language skills. Of the three groups, the first and by far the largest was dominated by subjects related to his chosen professional field: more than half (twenty-two classes in all) of his course work was in subject areas specifically related to business.

The second group includes eleven courses (six of them are related to business or accounting as well), including introductions to government, psychology, and economics, among others. In contrast, the third group includes nine classes related to reading, writing, and speaking, spread out over a two-year period. Among these: a first-year introduction to the library; two semesters of English composition; two courses entitled Introduction to Fiction, Drama and Poetry; and a class in public speaking for professional people. During the summer of 1949, a year before he graduated, he completed his English course work with one section each of Business Letters and Business Reports. As might be expected, courses related to his major in commerce occupied much of his time in college. Yet it is also true that outside of his professional specialization, English-language skills were placed on an equal footing with all other fields in the liberal arts. If we were to include the business-related survey courses of the second group with the business-specific courses of the first, he studied only five classes outside of the field of business unrelated to work in the English language. Two of his English-language courses were related to business as well.

Outside his specialty, his curriculum demanded familiarity with several sorts of knowledge as well as an in-depth study of a variety of subject areas related to the English language. Each semester included an introduction to a new academic field, classes in his main area of interest, and, importantly, ongoing work in the English language. In effect, the English language was a sort of de facto minor to his major in commerce. A majority of these courses were outwardly pragmatic and skills-oriented (the library class, the composition courses, and the business reports and letters classes), but the two introductory courses in literature were ostensibly more related to the aims of a liberal education. Given my father's economic and social background, then, it makes sense that it would be the pragmatic classes that would have the most immediate and long-lasting impact on his own literate practices. What did English studies have to say about what it meant to be a literate, middle-class man in the United States?

Literary studies has typically been seen as signifying certain existential and even nationalist educational practices and ideals; in contrast, the study of language as such is often understood as emphasizing vocational purposes, crossing from training in the basics of analytic reading to technical writing instruction to forensics. Historically, the sorts of literacy that played such an important role in my father's life were defined by academics as less important than what David Russell calls the "new ideal of research, of knowledge for its own sake," that most recalls his desires for his children (107). For my father, it seems, these distinctions were translated into a potential transformation of sensibility that he believed would reach fruition only in his children's lives. He would make the initial move into the middle class, but this would be a transition that in some sense would be completed only by the next generation. Class, for my father, was not simply about money; the finances could be achieved in a generation, but the sensibility required the secure childhood he had not had.

This differentiation between the aims of literature and that of composition, nonetheless, is not absolute. As Russell notes, until recently, writing instructors (often students of literature) most often relied on a "belles lettres" approach that embodied a kind of resistance to the pragmatic goals associated with vocational pedagogy (107). Richard Ohman has shown that this blurring of the pedagogic boundary between composition and literature was especially pronounced after the 1940s, when the New Criticism became the dominant literary mode of analysis (ix). In fact, literature and composition as fields of study have long shared important formulations of their pedagogical tasks and methodologies. Teaching literary close reading, for example, can approach the more or less formulaic stipulations of instruction in business writing.

Indeed, John Hagge, among others, contends that the conventions of business writing and communication courses, often thought of as constituting an independent tradition, are "in fact commonplaces of a 2000-year-old rhetorical tradition" ("Spurious Paternity" 34). Speech and composition classes, inasmuch as they focus on persuasion and ethos, offer instruction in our roles as individuals and as citizens. Business writing, literature, and composition courses can rely on exemplary models and normative descriptions to define successful texts. Almost any literature class requires some writing, and courses in composition inevitably rely on reading and rest on some notion of self, audience, and the purposes of texts.

Arguably, composition and literature are both composed of a dynamic mix of skill and sensibility. Why, then, have literary studies and composition traditionally occupied such different places in English studies? How should this disciplinary history shape an analysis of the accumulation of literacy as a form of cultural capital? As I noted earlier, I will return to an extended discussion of the relationship between class mobility and literary pedagogy in chapter 3. At this point, however, I would like to look at my father's textbook, *Unified English Composition*, in hopes of illustrating how composition pedagogy, as embodied in a popular textbook, can be seen as a methodology of class transformation seeking to teach key lessons about objectivity and language and about the merits of hard work in writing. These rhetorics of merit and professionalism lie at the center of the ideologies shaping education as an avenue to class mobility.

UNIFIED ENGLISH COMPOSITION AND THE RHETORIC OF OBJECTIVITY

Unified English Composition (*UEC*) opens with an "Orientation," in which students are given the fundamentals of college writing, beginning with the "Form and Appearance" of the manuscript and ending with a section on reading. The next four sections—on grammar, words, sentences, and paragraphs—introduce students to an analytic approach to language and work up to increasing levels of linguistic complexity. "The Whole Composition" next focuses on what James Berlin calls the "forms of discourse" (*Writing Instruction* 21), including chapters on exposition, the research paper, the feature article, biography, the book review, the informal essay, description, narrative, and the letter. The rhetoric of *UEC* emphasizes exposition and considers persuasion suspect, at the least.

Discussing the difficulties of understanding the intended meaning of abstract words, for example, the authors polemicize against behavior unbecoming to a professional. "Professional publicity writers and propaganda experts," they caution readers, "find it easy to influence the opinions and arouse the emotions of those who are not aware of the dangers [of] abstract terminology" (Sanders, Jordan, Limpus, and Magoon [hereafter *UEC*] 22). Words that "refer directly to things in nature, or to simple experience with nature," are the least likely to be misunderstood and so are the least litigious choice. "Thus, a chair is a piece of furniture, usually with four legs, designed to be sat in; we would all agree with that" (22). Persuasion is associated with the tribulations of miscommunication and subjectivity, if not the willful abuse of discursive power, and exposition with consensual understanding and objectivity.

The chapter on exposition offers an ethos of writing arising out of the assumed common experiences of educated professionals: "At every turn an educated person is called on to define, to explain, or to interpret something. Even if he would, he cannot escape answering such questions as: How is that made? What is such and such a thing or term? What are the facts about something? What are the aims of this book or that organization?" (271). Educated people must learn to write, in other words, because once they know the answer, they cannot help but try to communicate what they know. This knowledge imposes an ethical obligation; it is wrong for one to withhold his or her expertise. The introduction to the research paper underlines the ethical imperatives of exposition: "A glance at professional journals in the library or on the desks of such people as physicians, lawyers, teachers and engineers, will show that the research paper is not merely a contrivance to plague undergraduates.

It is the standard method of communication in any field of activity where the organizing of accurate information is important" (457). Imagine, the authors imply, a doctor who sloppily researches the possible medical remedies for an affliction or an engineer who skips over the arduous chores of calculating metal fatigue. Exposition is at the heart of the enterprise of learning to write in college and of the student's professional and moral obligations, because concise communication is the purpose of knowledge as such. Once you know, you have an obligation to tell. We learn not in order to persuade but in order to understand. To paraphrase Marx, the purpose of composition is to describe the world, not to change it.

This rhetorical emphasis on understanding (and explication) over persuasion (and argumentation) is important because whereas persuasion implies a degree of individual bias, understanding reinforces the ideal of an objective reality captured in language. Discovery, as Berlin notes in *Rhetoric and Reality*, is essential: meaning is found and then expressed, not created in process (6–8). The writer does not invent or design meaning but rather transmits it, and the expression of this truth is the central problem of the student as professional-to-be. *UEC* contends that "a body of knowledge is never brought to its most concise and valuable form until it is transmitted into writing" (3). Thus, *UEC* authors argue, even if one comes to school fluent in English, precise grammatical knowledge is crucial:

> Even the person who has always heard perfect grammar by those with whom he has associated, and who can usually distinguish a correct from an incorrect form merely by deciding what sounds right, needs to learn grammar. For all of us, the study of grammar, the systematic description of the ways of the English language, is necessary before we can be sure that what we speak or write is correct. Grammar . . . is a set of tools for shaping one's language into a correct and logically sound medium of expression. (50)

Intuition is not enough any more than it is for the scientist who must do more than simply sense that something is true. Science must provide shareable evidence. Effective exposition based on objective standards can itself do the work of persuasion; scientists know because they have seen the facts. Grammar, arising out of the scientific study of "the ways of the English language," provides objective proof of the propriety of Standard English. Science has demonstrated the importance of learning to write in college, the authors argue, and "investigation after investigation, each carried on with scientific objectivity, proves the truth of it" (10).

As in any profession, the writer must undergo a difficult apprenticeship, learning the value of hard work, efficiency, and dedication:

> If you come to see that learning to use your language correctly, effectively, and beautifully is important to you, you will face the drudgery and labor which in some part such a course entails. If you make the course [in Freshman English] what it is intended to be—a foundation for all your work—you will find that it will do you service during all your years as a student and afterwards as long as you live. (5)

The order of the list of adjectives expresses the hierarchy of values: one aims to write correctly and thus beautifully. In addition, effective writing requires the widest familiarity with the available tools of the trade, as it were, and so vocabulary is indispensable. The authors quote Johnson O'Connor on the efficacy of the acquisition of a wide vocabulary:

> An extensive knowledge of the exact meanings of English words accompanies outstanding success more often than any other single characteristic which the Human Engineering Laboratories have been able to isolate and measure. The balance of the evidence at the moment suggests that such a consciously, even laboriously, achieved vocabulary is an active asset. (qtd. in *UEC* 2)

Again, it is science, here of "Human Engineering," that warrants this ideology of language acquisition and so justifies the work of learning vocabulary. Science, in turn, is itself warranted by the ideals of merit in a democratic society. A rhetoric of persuasion, in contrast, must recognize that language is always at least partially shaped by subjective bias and that meaning is co-created in a complex interaction between writer, audience, and text. Berlin calls this view a "transactional theory" of language. In addition, Berlin argues that, while non-objective rhetorics have always been present in composition theory, they did not reach a position of real influence until well after the 1940s (*Rhetoric and Reality* 15). An "objective" rhetoric, however, rationalizes communication as a more or less simple matter of understanding what tools are available and which are necessary given the task at hand, then employing them to accomplish factual communication. If students are defined as co-producers of meaning, an entire array of complexity arises, not least of which is the formal properties of language. As professionals in the making, however, who must locate and employ objective knowledge, the task is simpler if no less arduous, and the student can remain a fundamentally passive recipient—and transmitter-to-be—of received knowledge.

The knowledge represented by *UEC* can be described as a hyper-rationalized model of the English language. The extensive use of lists, rules, and schematics reinforces the conflation of fluency and professional expertise. Grammar is relentlessly divided and then subdivided again in what seems an infinite series. The sections describing nouns, pronouns, adjectives, verbs, adverbs, and infinitives all include instructions for diagramming. Words are broken down into "three main classes of terms (exclusive of prepositions, conjunctions, and interjections)" (21). Usage has six levels (common, literary, technical, colloquial, slang, and illiteracy). Prose discourse has four forms—again, perhaps in order of importance ("exposition, argumentation, description, and narration") (331).

Essay types include formal and informal; biography entails character and biographical sketches as well as autobiography; letters include friendly letters and formal notes (and formal notes are divided into business, claim letters, and the letter of application). *UEC* offers a plethora of lists and rules, the latter in particular, presumably, to be memorized. These include, among others, suggestions for writing (128, 187, 292, 643) and for research papers (484); rules governing prefixes (142), suffixes (143), and the spelling of the plurals of nouns (143); a list of spelling words (144); a glossary of trite phrases to be avoided (172) and a glossary of faulty usage (175); a list of common abbreviations (483); and fifty ideas for newspaper features (508). The lists, of course, are a part of the rhetoric of expertise and objectivity, a knowledge too exhaustive, if not exhausting, to be acquired by the amateur and too complex to be used by the uneducated. Writing and rhetoric lie at the intersection of objectivity, merit, and professional expertise.

THE HARD WORK OF WRITING

The notion of hard work implicit in the rationalization of language plays an important ideological role in *UEC*'s description of the work of learning to write. In a meritocracy, social status is just insofar as it is earned. The harder one works, the more one earns, and an investment of time and effort into the accumulation of cultural capital yields the profits of increased status. The laborious work of language requires, too, that *UEC* offer frequent warnings about the necessity for vigilance; improper grammar can have disastrous personal, professional, social, and even economic effects. Many definition problems, the writers explain as if to reassure students, can be resolved with a dictionary. As might be expected, *UEC* offers advice on buying and using this important tool, noting, "A good dictionary is one that is written accurately and scientifically" (130).

In the end, however, the meaning of words is arbitrary, even if assigned through a variety of objectively valid historical and social processes rather than by individual decision or whim. This is a particularly acute problem with abstract terminology:

> If someone disagrees with us as to what hospitality means, or has never heard of the word and wants to know about it, we cannot go and point to hospitality and say, "*This* is what we mean." Since we cannot refer to any concrete experience to check out the meaning of . . . abstract words, but are dependent on a kind of gentleman's agreement concerning them, they are the source of much grief. (21–22; emphasis in original)

This "gentleman's agreement" on the meaning of words extends to the choices of specific terms. These decisions, *UEC* argues, depend especially on social circumstances and demand a precise understanding of slight nuances of meaning. For instance, the authors discuss the coloration of synonyms of the word "walk," emphasizing that nuance reflects precision:

> In choosing a synonym . . . one can choose from plod, trudge, tread, stride, saunter, meander, hike, tramp, stroll, march, ramble, prowl, hobble, and sneak. Looking over this list, one realizes how general is the meaning of walk, and much care must be taken in selecting a suitable synonym. Some of the words suggest leisurely movement (saunter, meander, stroll); others, furtive movement (sneak, prowl). Still others are suggestive of people's personalities: an effeminate person minces, a military man marches, a conceited individual struts. (134)

The meanings of words are based in the "gentleman's agreement" of social convention, and the assigning of meaning is as logical as the gentlemen scholars themselves. The existence of an objective world—measured, defined, expressed—means that mistakes, misrepresentations of fact, are possible. Language, in short, is a human institution (unlike the objective world) and, like all human institutions, is subject to errors that the student and the professional must avoid. There is an objective world out there, and the struggle for an accurate representation of it is central to the human enterprise.

If what Bourdieu calls the popular ethos dominates *UEC* in every way, the beautiful nevertheless has its place. The beautiful, or what might be more accurately called the non-useful, is associated not simply with the formalist aesthetics of style but with social, non-quantifiable knowledge generally. The study of rhetoric, the authors contend, while grounded in the necessity for precision and efficiency in communication, embraces the cultural traditions of the educated middle class:

> Practicing engineers, for example, are increasingly demanding that the engineering college provide more and better training in English, even at the expense of technical training. President Day of Cornell University, in addressing the engineering body of this

> institution, made the following statement: "I should like to see them masters of the mother tongue, understanding the nature of human relationships, aware of what is going on in the social world, and sensitive to their cultural heritage." He has expressed the feelings of countless leaders of prominence and foresight. (4)

Again, mastery of the "mother tongue" must come before both specialized technical knowledge and the students' "understanding . . . of human relationships," the "social world," and "their cultural heritage." The useful is the foundation on which the beautiful—the non-useful, but still unavoidable—is constructed.

UEC's lists, schematics, and rules provide a framework into which the authors have inserted a variety of texts that serve to illustrate and reinforce the social and linguistic values of a prescriptive grammar. Each text is introduced briefly in the context of the lesson under discussion, and many are followed by exercises. The section on verbals is illustrated with the essay "Some Participles I Have Met" by Eugene S. McCarthy and concludes with a series of seven "Suggestions for Study" (123). Although some belles lettristic selections are included (Twain, Macaulay, De Maupassant, and the like), the texts are said to be chosen primarily for their professional relevance:

> No effort has been made to select purple patches or to represent only the best that has been written. Many selections are from contemporary periodicals, and are the sort of writing which students may well hope to equal in their own work. We are not among those, however, who believe nothing old is good; hence we have tried to make a judicious selection from the older writers as well as contemporary ones. (v)

The purple patches of (literary, aesthetic) prose are to be avoided both because they represent texts or desires with other than expository purposes and because they are unrelated to the narrowly defined goals of professional education.

In addition, as elsewhere, the standards of students' writing are defined in terms of objective processes of validation; the order of adjectives suggests the hierarchy of values:

> Few who study freshman composition will ever be professional writers; hence such a course does not aim primarily at training students to become creative artists, but to use their language effectively in the ordinary affairs of life. . . . The rules and practices employed in all forms of writing are not the result of some individual's idiosyncrasies, but have been accepted for reasons of logic, convenience, common sense, or good taste. (5)

Interestingly, creativity is equated with the professionalization of writing and with a level of craft that the student is unlikely to find necessary or to achieve. This too reflects a curriculum in which writing in particular, and communication in American English generally, comes first and more often than literary studies. Here, as elsewhere, the emphasis on professional expertise, defined as an ethos rather than an aesthetic, takes precedence.

This is not to say, however, that *UEC* completely ignores issues of style or the necessity of understanding an audience: "The research paper need not be dry as dust, a dull mosaic of quotations. If the student is interested in the topic which is chosen, there is no reason why he should not write as entertainingly as he does in any other assignment" (457). Writing, the *UEC* authors suggest, can best reach its audience if it reflects the writer's original engagement through drawing on emotions associated with a pleasurable activity. Interest, moreover, is closely associated with efficiency and with social propriety. In a selection titled "Dr. Johnson on Tediousness," James Boswell tells the story of Johnson's reaction to an overly long narrative whose simple point was that "the Counsel upon Shrewsbury were much bitten by fleas" (661): "Johnson sat in great impatience till the gentleman had finished his tedious narrative, and then burst out (playfully, however), 'It is a pity, Sir, that you have not seen a lion; for a flea has taken you such a time, that a lion must have served you a twelvemonth'" (qtd. in *UEC* 662). The counsel could have more simply and efficiently communicated his point; his slip undermines the transmission of fact, which ought to be his goal, and distorts the importance of his message, reflecting poorly on his character and status.

In every way, then, *UEC* embodies the values of the emerging American professional middle class, especially those social values set out by Lynn Z. Bloom in 1996: self-reliance, responsibility, respectability, decorum, propriety, moderation and temperance, thrift, efficiency, order, cleanliness, punctuality, delayed gratification, and critical thinking. In *UEC*'s representation of the struggle for cultural nobility, the useful would contain the beautiful; the authors assume, of course, that this struggle has already been won. What's more, as an objective rhetoric, *UEC* contends that the concise communication of the external world is a moral and ethical necessity of the educated citizen.

UEC, in Hagge's terms, is "anthropologically complex" ("Early Engineering Textbooks" 442) in that it is linguistically prescriptive and concerned with the preservation—if not creation—of what the *UEC* authors term "a man's breeding and social grace" (2). Hagge's study is based on textbooks published between 1910 and 1925. *UEC* was first published in 1942, but as I hope will become evident, it represents no radical break in the traditions Hagge discusses. In "A Foreword to Students," the authors contend that good writing must prioritize accurate communication, but that what is communicated is not simply thought:

> Bad grammar, faulty sentence construction, and incorrect diction are to be avoided because they may hinder precise transmission of thought from one mind to the other, but perhaps even more particularly because they possess a bad connotation. The college graduate who uses such expressions as "I ain't," "he don't," or "I can't hardly," is frowned upon not because he cannot be understood, but simply because educated men and women do not employ such expressions. To use them makes you as suspect as if you were to wear high yellow shoes to a formal ball. (2–3)

The "breeding and social grace" that would avoid the "bad connotation" of improper usage is important insofar as it is useful in effective (accurate) communication. In this sense, a "useful" grammatical knowledge said to facilitate the "precise transmission of thought" is given pedagogical dominion over the "breeding and social grace," which justifies the importance of avoiding "bad grammar, faulty sentence construction, and incorrect diction." The student's first concern ought to be linguistic propriety, and the social effects necessarily follow. What is most beautiful socially is what is most useful linguistically: the clear expression of ideas (and of social status) through a proper grammar. The aesthetic pleasure of a professional report or official letter as well as its social efficacy lie in its crisp conveyance of thought and steadfast adherence to grammatical propriety.

PROFESSIONAL WRITING

The following letter, dated June 10, 1966, in which my father sought to correct the Veterans Administration's record of his date of birth, can serve as an introduction to the principles of his writing practices. I quote the text in full, preserving its paragraph format:

> Dear Sirs:
>
> The attached birth certificate will confirm that my age was overstated when I applied for my insurance. This is because I lied about my age when going into the service.
>
> According to my computation, I have paid in premiums approximately $33.00 more than I would have paid had my age been correctly stated.
>
> I would appreciate your making all the necessary corrections and applying the refunds for overpayments to future premiums.
>
> Yours truly,
> James R. Watkins

Although there was a minor economic motive behind the text—the thirty-three dollars in overpayments—it's written impersonally and seeks to speak "truly," and objectively, as the closing of his letter suggests. It is directed toward correcting an administrative record rather than explaining or apologizing for my father's actions.[1]

The tone is unemotionally polite, precise, and direct, almost to a fault. Consistent with the rhetoric of objectivity of *UEC*, the text's apparent purpose is strictly expository, and its formal properties, such as they are, focus the reader's attention on content rather than on form. My father makes no attempt to dramatize the circumstances of his life and thus provide some persuasive force to his request. The language is grammatically precise ("$33.00 more than I would have paid had my age been correctly stated") and semantically minimal ("This is because I lied . . . when going into the service"). It seeks simply to report a fact and to request action. The emphasis on grammatical accuracy and exposition as well as wariness toward persuasive and emotional language are also characteristic of *UEC*. This ethos of writing and professionalism is consistent with the writing my father did at his job in the public services department of the city of Houston.

In the midst of a telephone rate controversy in the summer of 1972, Steve Singer, a staff writer for the *Houston Chronicle*, summed up my father's professional tasks: "His job is to study Ma Bell's operations, expenses and income, and then make a recommendation to City Council on the telephone rate increase" (1). Noting the ferocity of the dispute—"the 'most bitter I have ever experienced,' says Councilman Frank Mancuso"—Singer vividly portrays my father as a writer and researcher:

> Reference books, pamphlets, magazines and phone company materials clutter his desk and nearby tables. An adding machine and an assortment of pipes and ashtrays take up what's left of the desktop. Pencils are visible everywhere. In Watkins' pockets, in his ear, on the desk, as page markers in the books, on the adding machine. His hands and face are smeared with graphite stains. Watkins has been gathering the rate material for years, probably since he began as a rate analyst with the Louisiana Public Services Commission in 1952. (1)

Singer presents my father's work as a long-term analytic research project—"Watkins has been gathering the rate material for years"—involving the location and interpretation of a complex range of legal, statistical, social, and economic data. "'It's very difficult to determine a rate base in Texas,' [Watkins] says, 'because State law requires taking into account inflation and technology and its effects.'" In addition, Singer notes, "Other factors . . . are working capital allowances, construction in progress, property held for future use and payments to affiliates" (3). "The man who'll have a major say in the telephone company's plea for a rate increase," Singer writes, "labors in a statistical jungle" (1). The effects of this work were literally all over my father's body: "His hands and face are smeared with graphite stains."

My father's report, "Rates and Research Major Activities 1972," further illustrates his professional emphasis on disinterested, objective fact and an implicit suspicion of persuasion as inherently self-interested. The memo opens with a depiction of the activities of my father's division:

> The primary function of this division is to supply technical information in the regulation of investor owned public utilities and certain other franchised businesses operating within the City of Houston. The goal is to maintain a continuous inspection and surveillance of all rates, fares, tolls and charges collected from the public by such utilities and to make studies of such rates from time to time in order to keep informed and to prepare reports. In the event of an application for a rate increase, it is the duty of this division to work on behalf of the public. (J. Watkins, par. 1)

Again, the language is grammatically precise and semantically succinct. The memo then details other department activities ("In 1972, monthly reports from Houston's major utilities . . . were reviewed"), suggesting that more such reviews were expected in the future ("A similar report on cost adjustments in gas rate schedules is now required from Houston Natural and United Gas" [par. 2]). Thus far, the report, as the title would indicate, is little more than a recitation of the tasks of the department. However, the text then shifts focus toward a more subtly persuasive agenda: "A proper analysis of these reports is time consuming to the rate analyst. The national fuel shortage problem created work for the division during this year. Both major gas companies were granted adjustment provisions in the Houston domestic rates" (par. 2). Again, the writer returns to the data—the costs and provisions of the contract with Houston Natural and United Gas—and concludes, "We should expect future increases" (par. 2). The next paragraph revisits the subject of workloads:

> A large part of the time of our Rate Analyst is spent answering inquiries and dealing with customer complaints. Telephone subscriber complaints were especially numerous in 1972. Part of the reason was due to an application by Southwestern Bell for a major rate increase. Consultants were employed by the City to study the need for this increase and to evaluate the quality of telephone service in Houston. (par. 3)

The report ends with fourteen "important assignments" and concludes, "Because of the work load of this department, consideration is currently being given to the employment of more rate analysts and/or auditors" (unnumbered par.). As in the letter, the prose is terse, even cursory. The language is emotionally neutral; the tone objective and dispassionate.

The memo has two themes. First, it accurately reports factual data, concentrating on a summary of the department's activities and on the relevant facts concerning the natural gas contract rates. The text's persuasive force fully rests on this carefully constructed tone emphasizing disinterest and objectivity. Second, the text hints at an ongoing or unfolding crisis: if, for example, complaints about Houston Natural and United Gas were to reach the proportions of current public criticism about Southwestern Bell, the division might be overwhelmed. It underlines this possibility by noting that "we should expect further increases" and by presenting a list of other activities that, given the possibility of public dissatisfaction, would strain the resources of the department. Numerous institutional reasons, of course, might be cited for my father's unwillingness to argue more passionately that his department was facing a crisis. This is only another way of saying that the ideology of professionalism and objectivity was an institutional imperative as well as an embodied disposition.

In the most general sense, too, "to be professional" means avoiding anything that might be seen as overly self-interested: the rationale of a professional report as such is careful balance and clear objectivity and exposition. Indeed, the impersonality of this ethos allowed my father to speak of himself in the third person, as "our analyst" rather than as a particular man, doing a particular task under specific (and trying) circumstances. In any case, what I would like to note here is that the objective purposes of the report—the citation of activities and facts—clearly dominate its persuasive tasks. In an objective text, as it were, the facts are meant to speak for themselves. Yet if, as my father suggests, the department was under pressure, the persuasive argument that more support was needed would seem to be at least an equally pressing task. In the piece from the *Houston Chronicle*, Singer describes my father's situation in the department in this way, hinting at some of the problems only implicit in the memo: "He [Watkins] has a secretary and the part-time help of city public services department director Tom Tyson. Another rate analyst retired two years ago and Tyson hasn't been able to find a replacement. 'We can't pay enough to attract one,' Tyson says" (1). Singer also reports that my father's supervisor was considering hiring consultants to assist in resolving the rate dispute and that it was difficult if not impossible to hire an additional CPA at current salary levels. "Watkins, 49, makes about $15,000 a year," Singer reports. A professional and objective rhetoric, however, demands that this nominally self-interested agenda must be rhetorically and linguistically downplayed, despite its wider implications for public policy. The phrases that signify the problems my father faced—"A proper analysis . . . is time consuming" and "A large part of the time . . . is spent answering inquires and dealing with customer complaints"—are without superfluous adjectives or adverbs. Understatement is its most significant trope.

As in his letter to the Veterans Administration, the purpose of this text is rhetorically straightforward and ethical, the truthful management of fact and the fulfillment of a professional duty. If it were to be judged aesthetically at all, it would be only to the extent that it efficiently accomplishes its communicative task without thereby calling attention to either its writer or its language. Readers are meant to look through, not at, the language. In the next chapter, I examine in more detail how this notion of language can be understood as a specific form of cultural capital. To understand the relationship of this ethos to *UEC*, we need to examine the broader social networks that shaped professional writing and composition pedagogy. Why did an "objectivist" rhetoric become the norm in both classroom and the workplace? How did this epistemology of language, which is, after all, only one epistemology among many, become so omnipresent as to seem not so much a force as a fact of nature? Why has what Berlin calls a current-traditional pedagogy so dominated writing pedagogy over the last half century? One answer lies in the complex desires for transformation and sociological change implicit in the relationships between education and class mobility. And in order to get at that complex system of want and need, I will have to return to my father's biography.

THE SILENCE OF THE MIDDLE CLASS

The basic facts of my father's life can be sketched out in just a few lines: He was born in rural Mississippi in the 1920s, joined the army in World War II, attended college on the GI Bill, married while in college, raised four children, and died in the early 1980s. In one way, his life was uneventful and modest in its accomplishments; in another way, it was extraordinary. He began his life as the son of a tenant farmer and ended it as an established professional. My father's story is in this sense resonant of that now perhaps too familiar tale of economic mobility and affluence often said to be typical of the American experience in the century just ended. Yet the significance of this series of transformations is not so easily summarized. Socioeconomic class, of course, is as much about sensibility and culture as it is about finance and so cannot be reduced to a set of neat economic facts. Still, these injunctions about getting an education are common, and the idea of reading and writing as a key to education and success is likely recognizable to almost any American teacher, parent, or student. What strikes me most, however, are the gaps between my father's own reading and writing practices and the dreams he had for what these skills ought to be for me.

Books were around when I was a child, but they never seemed central to my parents' lives. The cramped, faltering bookcase that stood in the hallway of our house in Houston contained only decades-old nonfiction hardbacks and textbooks from about the time of my father's undergraduate degree, more than fifteen years earlier. In the living room we had a complete set of the 1964 edition of the *World Book Encyclopedia*; on the coffee table in the den and on the headboard of my parents' bed, there were always a few more-or-less recent copies of *Reader's Digest*. Occasionally I might find my mother browsing through magazines or reading the church bulletin, and my father certainly read and wrote memos and reports at his job as a CPA for the city, but I cannot once recall either of them reading even a mass-market novel. They received and sent very few personal letters of any kind. They were literate, of course, but reading and writing were never essential to my sense of them and the kind of life they lived.

Still, my father always encouraged me to read as much and as widely as possible; the one exception to his habitual financial prudence was that he bought books for me whenever I asked. I was his only son, and not surprisingly he took a special interest in my education; when it came to books, cost was not an issue. Otherwise, while we never did without, as my mother says, there were few luxuries. The family television was an old black-and-white set that my parents had brought with them when they moved from Louisiana; my father bought only two new cars before his death in 1982. As a family, we rarely went out to dinner, to the movies, or on vacation.

I remember the front of our house always seeming to have more than one color of paint; to my eyes it was the least well-kept on our block. I felt both ashamed and proud of our house, which despite its faults seemed to suggest some subtle yet vital difference between my family and the rest of the neighborhood. Even so, when my father came home in the evenings, he was often carrying a book for me that I imagined he had found while perusing the newsstand at City Hall. As I grew older and he learned my preferences, these were usually science fiction best-sellers; once, when I was in the hospital for a minor operation, he gave me *Tom Sawyer*. I have always enjoyed writing and being a writer, which my father once told me was fine, as long as I did not end up a suicide like Hemingway.

Given the poverty he knew as a child, it might seem unlikely that a man like my father so strongly encouraged me to read without restriction and later so fully endorsed my outwardly impractical choice of an undergraduate major in English. One might expect that economic security would be an overriding concern in his hopes for his son; it was certainly at the heart of his own educational and social aspirations. Books, after all, are hardly essential, and a college degree is expensive and time consuming. But the idea of a college degree, as I understood his instructions, was to be educated first and then, using what I learned about myself and the world, to choose a job. I don't recall him ever speaking to me of a "career"—that's not a word that came to him readily. But implicit in his vision of my future was the idea of an education as a way forward financially and personally, and reading and writing would make it all possible. A college degree, for my father, was about more than earning a living; it was an invitation to move beyond the boundaries of his own childhood.

My father wanted something more for his son's life, and that something more was intimately related to education in general and to language in particular. Reading and writing were for him tools to be used at work, to stay informed about current events, to communicate now and then with a distant relative, conceivably a way to relax. He went to school in order to get a better job and to earn more money, and little in his everyday habits afterward made his college experiences appear all that important in adult life. Certainly, in college he learned the skills and practices he would rely on to support his family. Just as obviously, his cultural sensibilities were rooted as much in his childhood as in the college classroom. Yet my father also taught me that an education was an open-ended, potentially transformative search for knowledge and self, a prerequisite to the choice of a job or a profession rather than the choice itself.

My father, in other words, taught me that an education could have an economic purpose—eventually, as in his case, to get a job as an accountant for the city of Houston—but also that it had social and personal implications well beyond the monetary. In a capitalist society, of course, no one fully escapes the market. Certainly, few working-class men of the 1940s could wholly ignore economic realities. Yet class mobility was, for my father, rooted as much in the experiences of reading and writing as in income, each a necessary but not sufficient condition for middle-class status and for a measure of security, economic and otherwise. My father understood that moving out of the working class could mean taking on a new way of understanding the world, a way of living that nonetheless remained just out of his reach. When he implored me to read, and later to go to college, in other words, he was asking me to do more than earn a degree; he was inviting me to take the next step in a transformation of life and self that he had begun many years earlier. The difficulty of narrating my father's life, then, as well as its value lie in the telling of this story of an ongoing evolution of sensibility and self, a change I believe was at least in part achieved through an education in English language and literature. This text is itself a moment in that evolution and so is as much about myself as it is about my father and my family.

My father's injunctions, in short, can be understood only in the context of his socioeconomic background and of his desire to move out of the working class. A certain linguistic sensibility as well as a rhetoric of professionalism lie at the heart of his college curriculum, his composition textbook, and his writing. Yet I would also like to articulate what my father believed I ought to be moving toward, as well as what he was leaving behind. And in reflecting on my father's aspirations, I must concede that I am expressing an important, if unspoken, dimension of my family's life. My father never wanted to be wealthy; the economic "middle" was achievement enough.

Indeed, one of the primary motifs of this study is that a middle-class status is by definition an ongoing process, less teleology of material success than an evolution of sensibility. It is this freedom to explore individual possibilities, not ostentatious financial success, that I would argue is essential to our traditional notions of the American dream. Less often acknowledged is that the everyday form of this dream is in fact about being middle-class, not simply achieving material success. Admittedly, of course, this freedom and its ethical correlations are as much hope as recognition on my part. Still, it is that sensibility, that desire for a world beyond mere necessity, that we address in our lessons to our students, even if we as a profession so rarely articulate our largest goals, aims that are economic and social, material and spiritual.

It's often been noted that Americans, academic or otherwise, rarely discuss class. As bell hooks has said, "Nowhere is there a more intense silence about class than in educational settings" (177). Our silence about class in the United States too often means we do not discuss what being middle-class ought to be culturally as well as financially, as opposed to what it too often is. This silence encourages the false notion that mere numbers can encapsulate the myriad desires and motivations that drive class mobility. Polite society finds talk of money inappropriate, surely, but it is also quiet on our other, less easily articulated ambitions. Was my father wrong in seeking to become middle-class? What was lost and what was gained in his achievement? As a professor of English, I would like to ask: In what sense is an education in language and literature an ongoing project that seeks to affect a new form of employment and a new kind of self? What is this portfolio of skills and sensibility that we wish to promulgate through our lessons in language and literature, reading and writing? If in helping my students become educated, I am also helping them to become middle-class, then I must ask: What does it mean to be a literate member of the American middle class?

Clearly, my father's education in writing provides one answer or set of answers to this complex question. My father's life and work are the precursors of the knowledge workers studied by Brandt. In this sense, becoming part of the middle class simply means moving from work that is largely physical to work that is largely intellectual. Indeed, my father was a part of the first generation of the modern U.S. middle class. As I have argued, too, being middle-class for his generation meant, in part, that he followed an ethos of professionalism rooted in a notion of objectivity that found persuasion suspect. My father became middle-class because he wanted to learn to do a certain kind of work, and, I would argue, his course distribution and composition textbook provided exactly that sort of guidance. This vocational impulse, however, as I hope to make clear, does not tell the entire story of his education. Indeed, he saw his skills as only the first step in a larger project. As his transcript illustrates, the other side of that project, insofar as it relates to language, included courses in literature. In the next chapter, then, I would like to turn my attention to a more precise definition of the cultural capital represented by my father's degree. At the heart of that capital, I contend, lies the complex relationship between literary studies and composition.

2

English Studies, Rhetoric, and Writing

> The social world is accumulated history, and if it is not to be reduced to a discontinuous series of instantaneous mechanical equilibria between agents who are treated as interchangeable particles, one must reintroduce into it the notion of capital and with it, accumulation, and all its effects.
>
> —Pierre Bourdieu, "The Forms of Capital"

THE ATOMIC BOMB: EDUCATION AND POSTWAR AMERICA

WHEN THE U.S. MILITARY dropped an atomic bomb first on Hiroshima and then on Nagasaki in August 1945, effectively ending World War II, my father was stationed in Germany and preparing for what he thought would be an inevitable and dangerous tour in the Pacific Theater. He rarely spoke of this period, but I have always suspected that his silence suggested that he was in some way involved in the closing of the concentration camps. In any case, no one really believed, he told me years later, that any single bomb could do so much damage and so quickly stop the Japanese. His discharge orders were the final proof that the rumors of the fantastic weapon were in fact true and that he would soon be going home. Within a few weeks, he was shipped back to the United States, where he moved in with his uncle Pops and aunt Bell in Baton Rouge, Louisiana. My great-uncle Pops could offer his nephew a job building houses.

One summer day just a few months after his return from Europe, Dad was helping put in a roof, and he got so hot he almost fainted and fell off. Then and there, he said, he decided to take advantage of the GI Bill and go to college. The problem was that he had never finished elementary school, much less high school. He was determined, however, and within a few months, he had convinced the military that a flood had destroyed his public school records and he was taking classes at Baton Rouge High School at night. He received his GED, and a year later he enrolled at Louisiana State University. As I have said, he decided on a degree in commerce instead of his first choice of law because his military service qualified him for only four years of support. In the end, he managed to finish his courses in just over three years, graduating in the summer of 1950.

For a man of my father's background, the decision to go to school was fraught with social and economic risks. Along with the financial and bureaucratic problems he faced, his extended family found his decision difficult to understand and maybe a little crazy. He had sent his sister Thelma money for college during the war, but she had dropped out when she got pregnant with her first child, Buddy, and married a truck driver, my uncle Milford Munn. My father, too, was mainly responsible for his institutionalized mother; his father was an often unemployed alcoholic living alone in New Orleans. Uncle Pops's second son, Pumpkin, enrolled at the same time as my father but dropped out after only a few weeks, finding college too difficult and, no doubt, too alien an environment.

My father could get a job in the growing postwar economy, but his time in school could make it difficult or even impossible for him to meet what were likely to become ever more pressing family responsibilities. The Social Security Act, passed in 1935, attempted to address these sorts of problems in a limited way, and payments to retirees began in 1942. Perhaps most important for my father's family, however, was that social security, as originally designed, had no provisions for mental health insurance. His parents were growing older, and neither could offer any assistance; at some point, he would likely have to largely support one or both of them. His extended family was getting on with their lives as best they could, and he had little if any immediate experience of professional life. He must have been thinking that, if he succeeded in college, he could earn a much better income in the end; his parents' problems surely were a lesson in the vicissitudes and dangers of working-class life.

He wanted a better job, but he also wanted a different way of life for himself. The obvious solution was school.

My father faced several important obstacles in his desire to transform his class status. Given his family situation, he had little social capital in the middle-class professional world. After leaving college, for example, he could not call on friends of his father to assist him in finding a professional position. His family, too, recognized that he risked squandering the working-class social capital my father did have, in the form of his relationship to Uncle Pops's construction business. This was in the years before Levitt and Sons revolutionized the mass production of houses, and so Uncle Pops was less an executive than a leader of a team of craftspeople. My father's main asset was his military service, which he could immediately cash in, as it were, in the form of a limited amount of college tuition and a negligible if livable stipend. He was at least minimally literate—he could read and write, and his military service demanded rudimentary calculation skills. Thanks to his military service, too, he could quickly acquire the institutional equivalent of a high school degree.

A college degree in no way guarantees employment, however, and after finishing at LSU in 1949, my father spent a decade looking for a job that would provide some kind of financial security for him and his family. In fact, his degree did not necessarily mean that he would be able to find a professional position in his field at all. After he graduated, he worked for a brief time as a railroad engineer and an insurance sales representative. In the early 1950s, he passed the state examination to become a Certified Public Accountant and took a job with the state of Louisiana. For several years, he and my mother lived a nomadic life as he moved from assignment to assignment in Shreveport, Lafayette, and New Orleans. My older sister, Cynthia, was born in 1957, I was born in 1958, and Lisa quickly followed me in 1959. In the early 1960s, Dad accepted a job with the city of Houston as a utility analyst. He drove in with Cynthia to find and rent a house, and my mother, pregnant with Lisa, took me on a train a few weeks later to meet him.

Within a year or two of our arrival in Texas, we had settled into a three-bedroom house in a suburban development built over what were once rice fields. My sisters (soon joined by Jill) were crowded into one none-too-large bedroom, but as the only boy, I had the third to myself. When Cynthia entered high school in the early 1970s, we added a new room and bath so that she could have some privacy. My mother, like many women at the time, quit work soon after she was married and never returned, even after her children were in school. She did graduate from high school, along with most of her six brothers and sisters, but education was an experience, she has told me, that she would not want to repeat. We never did without, again to quote my mother, but in many ways my parents didn't take advantage of what many might consider the obvious financial and professional opportunities available to them. In particular, my mother, unlike many of the wives of professional men of the time, chose not to pursue her own career. This choice, perhaps as much as any other, meant that my family was never securely middle-class; we occupied a kind of practical-minded borderland just comfortably beyond living hand-to-mouth.

My father stayed at the same job until his death in 1982; he received incremental increases in salary but never changed positions. A better job, he would tell me, would only make him professionally dependent on the current mayor and so subject to the vicissitudes of electoral politics. By the mid-1970s, he was in some demand as an expert witness in utility rate disputes and was at least twice offered more lucrative jobs at the federal and state levels. He was hardworking and honest and seemed to earn a fair amount of professional respect, social capital that he could likely have used to move to a better job and so to a higher income. Yet he turned down each of these offers, arguing that the higher salary could not justify the inherent insecurity such a move would have on his family.

This financial reticence was consistent at all levels of his economic life. He used credit cards only rarely, which he quickly paid to avoid interest charges. He was sensible to a fault in the clothing he wore, owning little besides his three or four gray or dark blue suits. He had little occasion for the few nice clothes he did own, and after his death I found a thirty-year-old heavy black winter coat in his closet, still in good enough condition for me to keep and use. My father never seemed to acclimate himself fully to his new status. He treated his position at the city as a job, and he seemed either to be unaware of or unwilling to use his financial or social capital to move himself and his family more deeply into the mainstream of middle-class life. There were limits, in some sense, to how far he would—or perhaps could—move out of his working-class background.

ENGLISH STUDIES AS CULTURAL CAPITAL

Through much of the twentieth century, the steady growth in university tenure-track teaching positions helped to guarantee that the so-called apprentice system was seen as both fair and economically viable. It was efficient in that it enabled large numbers of students to be brought into the university at a relatively low cost; it was fair in that what was felt by many to be the sacrifice of teaching writing was compensated in the long term. Senior faculty, of course, could focus exclusively on advanced literary courses. In contemporary jargon, this system was scalable, capable of expansion and contraction as access to education grew and shrunk. The accessibility made possible by these institutional arrangements enabled a much wider distribution of cultural capital, helping to set the stage for the ongoing expansion of an economy dependent on middle-class labor. Literary education, however, because it was more expensive, was concentrated in the upper-course levels, where the smaller numbers of students could keep costs down and value up. In this sense, composition served as a filtering mechanism; access to literary forms of cultural capital was licensed by demonstrated degrees of competency in more utilitarian forms of writing. The relative rarity of access to literary education was dictated by the challenges of composition. Indeed, the certificate of a passing grade in freshman writing became a pass enabling the students to further their education in any field.

The rhetorics of objectivity, merit, and professionalism that shaped my father's writing practices cannot tell the entire story of his education in language. As I have emphasized, while he saw his own educational goals as primarily vocational, he had broader aspirations for his children's education. If he went to college to become middle-class by learning the ways and means of a profession, his children would go for transformative reasons associated with the liberal arts generally and with the study of literature specifically. I would argue that these closely related sets of educational goals are reflected in the distribution of language study courses in my father's curriculum. In this chapter, I define the cultural capital of English studies in a more precise way by drawing on the work of Pierre Bourdieu. In particular, I contend that the linguistic values implicit in English studies—here taken to mean both first-year composition and subsequent literary classes—have to be seen in terms of a mutually defining dialect of ethos and aesthetic.

I set the stage for my discussion of the cultural capital of English studies through a historical portrait of the emergence of the rationalized university—in effect, a broader example of the rationalization of language so prominent in *Unified English Composition.* I begin this narrative with a close look at a speech given by the publisher of *UEC*, Frederick S. Crofts, and then move into a more detailed discussion of the evolution of the university as seen by Clyde W. Barrow. Crofts provides an illuminating glimpse into the rationales surrounding textbook production and sales, a kind of reasoning echoed in the institutional transformations discussed by Barrow. Here, too, we find further explanations for the central role played by what James Berlin has called a current-traditional rhetoric. Far from a recent phenomenon, Barrow shows that the corporatization of the university in the United States has its roots in the early twentieth century. This corporatization, in turn, played a decisive role in shaping the cultural capital of English studies, particularly its emphasis on objectivity and its distrust of persuasion.

In this chapter, I explore how the rationalization of the university system, with its attendant rise in student population and maturation of a textbook market, was underpinned by the progressive values of its era. In particular, I show how the ideology of language represented in the English department created a merit-based hierarchy in which greater numbers of students would be exposed to an ethos of composition than to the aesthetics of the literary classroom. In this way, the uneven distribution of cultural capital could be explained in terms of talent and effort; hard work rather than inheritance would be the hallmark of the emerging middle-class system of education.

As I hope to make clear, the complex relationships between composition and literary studies have too often been ignored in favor of a disciplinary approach. These separate histories, represented here by the work of Terry Eagleton and James Berlin, while valuable in many ways, too often oversimplify our views of English studies. I conclude with an exploration of Bourdieu's conceptions of the popular ethos and the formal aesthetic as a more systematic framework in which to understand English studies. Literary studies and composition together make up what might be thought of as an idealized linguistic sensibility concerned with the practical matters of communication as much as with art.

THE RATIONALIZATION OF THE ENGLISH DEPARTMENT

Frederick S. Crofts, the publisher of my father's textbook, *Unified English Composition*, began his career in publishing as a sales representative at the Century Company just after the turn of the century and was promoted to manager of its educational department by 1910. In 1919, he moved to Harpers, where he specialized in educational textbooks. In the mid-1920s, he founded F. S. Crofts and Co., which by World War II had grown into one of the largest academic publishers in the United States. In the early 1940s, Crofts spoke at the annual Bowker Lectures on Book Publishing, sponsored by the New York Public Library. His speech, "Textbooks Are Not Absolutely Dead Things," was published in 1943 as part of that organization's Typophile Chap Book Series edited by Frederick G. Melcher. In a brief introduction, Crofts is described by the editors as "known and respected on every college and university campus across the country. . . . Crofts' books, always particularly well designed, now include 500 titles covering every field of college study" (78).

In his speech, Crofts argued that the ongoing expansion of the university system and the resulting intensified competition among publishers changed the industry in fundamental ways, encouraging publishers to focus on the presentation of their product, at times at the expense of its content. "In the formal educational period of most of us," Crofts said, "there was little or no attempt made by authors or publishers to appeal . . . to the emotions and . . . the aesthetic tastes of the reader." Crofts's talk illustrated these changes demographically:

> At that time [the early part of the century] there were less than 350,000 college students (today the number exceeds 1,300,000). A publisher's salesman of that day, when visiting a college, would be greeted with the statement that he was the first representative who had called in many months. In contrast today, fifteen or more are not infrequently found on one campus in a single day. (81)

Crofts noted that this period saw the creation of the first publishing departments dedicated to the acquisition and marketing of college textbooks (81).

More important, Crofts issued a warning about a trend toward "subjective" treatments of knowledge, especially in sociological textbooks. Crofts described this shift in terms of a move away from "the traditional weighing of evidence without personal bias to a subjective treatment generally towards the liberal and, not infrequently, the extreme left" (89). The publisher's task, Crofts believed, was to balance market sensitivity with attention to quality, which he associated with attractive but not overwhelming packaging on the one hand and with an objective treatment of the subject matter on the other. For Crofts, objectivity was outside of politics, neither left nor right, and the appeal to "emotion" represented by more attractive packaging was simply a matter of creating a more effective appeal in the market.

As a publisher, then, Crofts was deeply concerned with the relationship between ethos and aesthetics, apprehensive that the latter would overcome the former. Crofts's formulation of the proper place of the popular ethos, as well as his suspicion of aesthetics and persuasion, shaped the pedagogy he advocated. What's more, any discourse that formulated this relationship differently was, he argued, by definition ethically suspect. In an era crossing both war and economic depression, any non-objective treatment of content tended toward the left, Crofts believed, and by implication represented a threat to the system of property on which the market rested. Crofts stressed that attractive packaging was important and that academic trends may come and go, but objective standards were a "duty [that] cannot be escaped" (80). While lamenting the "subjective" bias of these newer texts, Crofts's worries were allayed by his belief that market influences had created a conservative inertia in college textbooks that resisted intellectual fashion. In addition, while the market shaped textbooks, the textbook publishers must also shape the market, insofar as they could resist this "subjective" bias. "Popular reading tastes influenced the trade," Donald Sheehan wrote in 1952, "as much as the trade influenced popular reading tastes" (22).

Crofts's sense of the duty of the publisher recalls James Berlin's description of the "objectivist rhetoric" that underlay what he terms "the most pervasive of objective rhetorics in the last hundred years and . . . the dominant rhetoric overall" (*Rhetoric* 9). Berlin believes this epistemology of language rests on the naive scientific faith that the "economical and political interests of the new professional middle-class were . . . inherent features of the universe" (37). Even more, Berlin writes, "since all truth was considered to be external to the individual, to be discovered through correct perception, the doctors or lawyers or engineers or business managers . . . felt that they were surely correct in discovering that economic and political arrangements that benefited them were indeed in the nature of things" (37). For Berlin, objectivity, in the form embodied in composition textbooks, was as much a matter of scientific method as of political and social self-justification. As a professional and a "trained observer," Crofts "saw" in the market a demand for textbooks whose assumptions reproduced a belief in the necessity and validity of his own class position. The professional textbook publisher produced textbooks that reiterated the objective validity of the social status of professionals, and Crofts's "duty," put bluntly, was to the reproduction and maintenance of his own class. Crofts's speech illustrates, among other things, a powerful concordance between an objective pedagogy of writing and an astute marketing sense.

At about the same time that Crofts was publishing his textbooks, universities in the United States underwent an extensive, if not often noted, institutional transformation, led by educational foundations and supported by the federal government. These reforms, as Barrow has shown, were achieved in a political climate in which pressures for increasing access warred with concern about costs and the aims of higher education more generally. Barrow notes that Samuel Gompers, among many others, called for "universal higher education" and suggested that "the vast majority would profit far more by some other kind of education than that given in the traditional American college" (96). The result of these "progressive campaigns for greater economy and accountability," according to Barrow, was that "colleges and universities became susceptible to the same kinds of judgments about their 'value' as any other institution" (97). Barrow calls these reforms "a significant ideological victory for business," which "displaced traditional metaphors and myths" (97).

Universities, like business, had to justify their work through a system of accountability judged by corporate standards:

> The progressive emphasis on the role of the expert meant that once educational questions were reformulated as problems of business organization and the investment of public capital, then presumably experienced businessmen—and not farmers, workers, students, or the general public—could rightly claim to be the experts. This created a scenario . . . in which not only did appointing businessmen to boards of trustees or educational reform commissions seemed legitimate, but in which doing the contrary would seem like mere "politics" instead of good public administration. (Barrow 97)

Barrow illustrates in detail how the managerial expertise presumed necessary was developed by "corporate intellectuals" and funded through organizations such as the Carnegie Foundation. The end result of these reforms included both an administrative cadre more distant from academic concerns and standardized methods of measuring institutional efficacy.

More important, Barrow also suggests why Crofts's marketing

strategies, as well as his pedagogy, found a responsive audience among professionals in education. Crofts was far from naive in his faith in objectivity. Writing of these "corporate reformers," Barrow notes:

> By linking the availability of increased financial resources for higher education to the adaptation of a corporate reform program, the foundations could use material pressures to reinforce the appeal of their proposed policy. They could, to quote Marx, represent their class interest "as the common interest of all society," and thereby plausibly claim that their ideas were "the only rational, universally valid ones." (75)

Publishers such as Crofts, drawing on the financial resources newly made available to universities, reinforced the foundations' goals and rhetoric through a marketing and educational ideology that, perhaps not surprisingly, relied on the progressive ideals of neutral objectivity. The high status of the research institutions encouraged the propagation of these ideas throughout the higher education system, a process reinforced by what John Hagge calls "scientific optimism" ("Early Engineering Textbooks" 440). Seeking to eliminate what was thought to be inefficient institutions, organizations such as the Rockefeller-funded General Education Board promoted a distinction between the university and the college "on the basis of graduate research and professional training leading to a post-baccalaureate degree" (Barrow 84). This rationalization, of course, made Crofts's task all the easier.

The subsequent rapid increases in the demand for education and the perennial lack of adequate public funding—then, as now—further reinforced the foundations' power to drive change. In effect, the objective educational philosophy was not simply a pedagogical necessity, given the increase in what were thought to be ill-prepared students, but also a political project consistent with the interests of the professional middle classes. "Presidents [of universities] with populist loyalties," Barrow writes, "or those who too strongly defended the claims of faculty members against governing boards, littered the decade of the 1890s" (78). In this context, Berlin's description of the pedagogical aims of "objectivist rhetoric" is worth quoting:

> Since language is arbitrary and enters into meaning only after the truth is discovered, the writer must take pains that language not distort. . . . Since it is to reproduce in the reader the experiences of the original observer, it must possess energy and vivacity. Finally, since language is to demonstrate the individual's qualifications as a reputable observer . . . it must conform to certain standards of usage, thereby demonstrating the appropriate class affiliation. (*Rhetoric* 9)

Language is a problem if used incorrectly, and the technicalities of grammar and syntax are taught in hopes of avoiding an inaccurate reproduction of the author's originating perception. Moreover, the ability to spell correctly, to be precise yet vivid and so to faithfully reproduce preexisting knowledge, and so on, is itself evidence of an educated, middle-class sensibility.

EDUCATION AND MERITOCRACY

Traditionally, it was assumed that students were eligible for college due to their social pedigrees (including race as well as gender and class). Pedigree in the nineteenth-century was what Lynn Z. Bloom has called a "closed loop" of class in which students were overwhelmingly male and came from white upper-class families and so went to overwhelmingly male and white upper-class universities (656). I'll return to Bloom's helpful descriptions at the end of the chapter. Here, I only want to emphasize that, in a democracy, the supporters of progressive meritocracy argued, this circuit of privilege must be broken. A rhetoric of objectivity and merit thus played a central role in the re-creation of the historic U.S. middle class. Arguably, of course, ongoing economic changes also made the breaking of this circuit inevitable. In any case, the ideology of a democratic educational system insists that social and economic backgrounds are largely irrelevant and that higher education ought to be made available to anyone with what *Unified English Composition* calls the "fair intelligence" needed to succeed in college (1). The ideal of the meritocracy, founded in "scientific optimism," both justified and enabled, on the most practical level, a rapid expansion of higher education while strictly regulating and limiting the distribution of cultural capital.

Necessarily, composition and literature differed in their roles, the former ensuring the relative scarcity of the latter. In theory, one might say, anyone willing to work hard was given the chance at becoming a member of the middle class; in practice, these opportunities were unequally distributed via the entire apparatus of testing and evaluation, which served as representations of achievement and potential. As my father's transcript illustrates, all students were given the opportunity to further develop a popular ethos, but far fewer were offered intensive exposure to the study of an aesthetic form of writing. The curriculum echoed the system of professional status: composition instruction was, in effect, "common" and thus poorly rewarded; literary studies was more rarified and, as such, was assigned more social and economic capital.

Historically, as the content of cultural capital grew more specialized and students' educational experiences increasingly decomposed into professional literacies and academic specialties, prescriptive language instruction remained both a unifying force and a key system of determining eligibility for what was thought to be the higher forms of knowledge. The objective rhetoric that dominated composition, then, is inseparable from the modern democratic project of the U.S. university system; its persistence is historically linked to the ongoing maintenance and reproduction of education. To the progressive ideology that founded it, composition ensured order in what was perceived to be a chaos of possible literacies.

An objective conception of language, then, sought to rationalize the irrationality of competing dialects; objectivity was thus closely associated with democratic access. As with administrative rationalization, linguistic normalization was accepted as both cost-efficient and supportive of democracy. The multiple hierarchies of the U.S. university system could be held together through the twin bonding apparatus of (linguistic and social) propriety and merit. In this sense, to be educated meant that one spoke a common, refined English and had earned—not inherited—the social and economic privileges aptly represented by one's command of the language. Some, of course, earned more than others, and in English departments, that excess was expressed in the aesthetic dimension of language. Conversely, of course, if one did not speak or write so-called refined English, one was said to be either unwilling or unable to accomplish the requisite work; failure collapsed into character. In this context, the English major best represents the underlying ideology of traditional English studies. What's more, the educational and scholastic ideology of individual initiative, whether on the part of administrations, teachers, or students, need not threaten the capitalist structure itself as long as the system of objective measurement (and merit) remained in place. Access to capital was seen as limited by character rather than by status.

In short, everyone could give it a shot, and quite "naturally" this resulted in an uneven distribution of cultural capital along class, race, and gender lines. Educational access could be nominally democratized—and professionalized—without a too equal distribution of capital; the potentially prohibitive cost of democracy in a heterogeneous society could be managed. For much of the twentieth century, this pattern would remain largely unchanged, a stasis well represented by the dynamics of the emerging market for the objective capital, the textbooks, that circulated through the education system. Arguably, the nominal "objectivity" peddled via composition textbooks represents the underlying social and economic ideology of the era, its weighting of science and democracy and capitalism embodied in a meritocratic faith in individual progress.

Indeed, to the extent that language played a central role in these ideologies, they document the crucial, if too often unrecognized, role of writing instruction in the creation of the U.S. middle class. These textbooks, as well as their publishers, embodied the tastes and values implicit in the ongoing rationalization of the university and the English department. My study thus suggests a central role for composition that for many might seem counterintuitive. In the traditional view, literary studies played the key role, while composition was relegated to the discipline's periphery. Clearly, literary studies had a higher academic status for much of the twentieth century. I want to argue, however, that composition lay at the heart of the educational goals of U.S. education in this period, particularly as they related to the personal and social transformations associated with widespread class mobility. Why has composition's important role been so often neglected?

ENGLISH STUDIES AS DISCIPLINE

As Henry A. Giroux has emphasized, all university course work contributes to an education in schooling as much as it does to learning in any specific knowledge area (5–8). In this sense, composition and literature have always been more alike than not. In marked contrast to Giroux, however, historical studies in English-language education have stressed the importance of the institutional and academic divisions between different forms of English language and literary instruction rather than their interactions or interrelationships. This focus on what might be called academic or disciplinary identity has served to understate the complex dynamics of the accumulation of literacy, downplaying both the contradictions and the similarities between differing modes of language instruction and accumulation. Yet the specific forms of cultural capital that have been historically distributed through English studies are defined precisely through this complex set of interrelationships. First-year writing and literary studies are mutually defining forms of linguistic cultural capital.

Terry Eagleton's *Literary Theory: An Introduction* and James A. Berlin's *Rhetoric and Reality: Writing Instruction in American Colleges, 1900–1985* can serve as examples of the missed opportunities, if not distortions, represented by a focus on disciplinary identity at the expense of a more dynamic view. Like David Russell, both Eagleton and Berlin argue that the intertwined history of university-level literary and composition studies in the United States reached a crucial turning point about the time of my father's degree. In a profound sense, English studies became synonymous with literary studies. Acknowledging this, however, both Eagleton and Berlin go on to focus almost exclusively on their respective disciplines, leaving aside any further analysis of the dynamics of the accumulation of literacy.

Is dominance the sole or even the most important factor shaping the historical relationship between literary studies and composition? Clearly, for my father, the vocational dimensions of his degree, rather than its liberal arts components, were of paramount importance. What's more, my father's transcript suggests an elaborate set of relationships between composition and literature that would be difficult to reduce to any straightforward pattern of academic or hierarchical authority. In a commerce degree, business courses are, by definition, central. In terms of class time, too, my father's composition, literature, and business-writing courses were given an equal emphasis. If literary studies was academically predominant by the time of my father's degree, that status was not expressed in any simple way through the distribution of English-language courses in his curriculum. Literature, in my father's transcript, was only one course among many that dealt with the English language. It was the study of the English language generally that played a dominant role in my father's degree, not literary studies specifically.

Berlin and Eagleton, of course, assume a historical process in which English-language studies decomposed into what became its constituent and, eventually, professionalized parts. In this way, "English" became "speech," "composition," "linguistics," "literature," "creative writing," and so on. Over time, and depending on circumstances local and otherwise, many of these subfields, like speech and linguistics, evolved into distinct fields, with physically and intellectually separate departments. English departments at midcentury commonly offered classes in composition and literature, with the latter said to be the most distinguished; rhetoric and composition were left to languish—or flourish—in the hands of graduate students and adjunct professors. This is what Russell refers to as "the triumph of specialization" (107). But beyond this common institutional history, Berlin's and Eagleton's stories diverge sharply.

Berlin's primary interest is in understanding how rhetoric reemerged as a modern academic field rather than in an examination of English-language education as such. His analysis takes the effects of schooling into account, at least implicitly, but his overarching concern lies with what he feels has been the neglected study of the epistemological evolution of writing pedagogy. Berlin would like to restore to rhetoric and composition some of the prestige once accorded to the traditional professor of rhetoric and so help to reformulate them as the equal of literary studies. The history of writing instruction, Berlin shows, is intimately connected to what he terms an objective ideology ideally suited to the worldview of the then emerging professional middle classes. As we have seen, this ideology shaped both my father's college textbook as well as the rhetorical assumptions of his professional writing. Berlin's main goal is to give composition an intellectual pedigree comparable to literary studies—that is, to overturn the latter's presumed dominant status.

Similarly, Eagleton's book is concerned with how literature and literary theory evolved into a discrete category of disciplinary thought aimed at reinforcing, if not establishing, an ideology that served to justify U.S. economic and cultural hegemony. In Berlin's terms, rhetorical instruction in the late 1940s would have centered more or less in an "objectivist epistemology" with its emphasis "on exposition—analysis, classification, cause-effect, and so forth" (*Rhetoric* 9). While gesturing to rhetoric's institutional siblings, and to literacy as the "center of the educational enterprise," Berlin's analysis is nonetheless aimed toward the progressive historical argument that rhetorical theory leads inexorably to its current "transactional" emphasis on the interdependency among writer, text, and audience (15). Eagleton frames his history in terms of the changing role of the United States in the world and of the consolidation and evolution of literature as an academic field. New Critical pedagogy, in Eagleton's view, is best understood in terms of its pivotal role in the institutional legitimization of literary studies. Literary theorists, critics, and teachers are not so much purveyors of doctrine, Eagleton argues, as curators and protectors of a discourse. In this sense, he implies, it hardly matters which theory is being promoted, at least as long as the institution of literary studies is sheltered.

As such, professors of literature have multiple roles: to preserve this discourse, to extend and elaborate it as necessary, to defend it from other forms of discourse, to initiate newcomers into it, and to determine whether they have successfully mastered it (Eagleton 201). By the late 1940s, Eagleton contends, the New Critics had secured a niche for themselves as the "custodians" of the literary culture of the American nation. The dominance of literature (within English departments) is, in this sense, a kind of institutional and academic analogy to the political dominance of the United States. Eagleton's central aim is to solidify our understanding of the historical relationships among ideology, national culture, and literature. Studies like his and Berlin's offer insights into the historical and professional landmarks in the wider network of an educational system. Eagleton is surely right that, as professionals, English professors have had to serve as guardians of their discipline. Indeed, as I hope to show in my discussion of the current debate over the future of English studies, many professors still see their role as primarily custodial.

Especially in the period just after World War II, nationalist pride in the achievements of U.S. culture colored many if not all curricula. It might be reasonable to assume that this nationalism is potentially present in any field or profession. Similarly, Berlin's typology of the pedagogy of rhetoric is accurate as a broad description of how a profession conceived of its own aims and purposes and how it secured a place for itself within academic institutions, however professionally tentative. Whether or not teachers "on the ground," as it were, actually adhered in every case to this typology is in all probability an unanswerable question. In the end, certainly, no analysis can claim full comprehension of any particular phenomenon, and Berlin and Eagleton cannot be faulted for making a choice about what seemed most important to argue to their colleagues. Nonetheless, in telling the story of English-language education as a narrative of their respective disciplines, Berlin and Eagleton have risked an oversimplification that, I would argue, has become endemic. Their approach severs their English from the broader context of an undergraduate education on the one hand and the accumulation of literacy on the other.

What is the relationship between my father's desire to improve his life, utilitarian language, and Berlin's narrative of composition's long search for legitimacy? How can we understand the ties among "research for its own sake," my father's wishes for his children, and literary studies' professional and disciplinary authority? In effect, Eagleton focuses on the higher-status professors, mostly male, and Berlin on the more typically female adjuncts. Ironically, each writer's interest in ideology as such enables a neglect of the mutual interdependence of adjunct and professor, in several senses. The adjuncts teaching first-year English are in one study; the professors teaching literature are in another. Neither explores the politics of employment. An investigation into literacy and ideology, in this sense, hides more than it reveals.

Each of their analyses, too, suggests that classroom instruction in English language and literacy occurs simply and directly from the top down, from instructor unproblematically into student. The professor seeks to instill national pride, so therefore the student must surely have internalized this love of country. In Eagleton's analysis, regional or ethnic pride, or class identification or aspiration, has no place. Again, neither he nor Berlin explores how these notions might be shaped by either the immediate context of the student's degree plan—in my father's case, commerce—or by the succession or accumulations of educational experiences brought to a university education by a student. Is a student from a working-class or poor background more or less likely to accept the messages—implicit or otherwise—embodied in a particular course of study?

Eagleton argues that national and even global forces played a central role in shaping literary studies; Berlin concentrates his attention on the internal debates of a profession as they occurred within the context of an era of reform and growth in the educational system. On one level, each seems to take into account agendas outside their respective fields of study; each affirms the importance of broader social and historical forces. Yet, at the risk of belaboring the point, in the case of my father's degree and in the context of his life, preserving American literature as such would not likely have been his most pressing pedagogical imperative. In the same way, we might wonder how apparent the illegitimacy of composition would have seemed to students only vaguely familiar with professional life of any sort. For a man like my father, fresh off the farm and then the battlefield, as it were, all teachers likely were equally mystifying, no matter their status. How can English studies be analyzed as a dynamic social process, in short, without neglecting either accumulation or schooling?

CULTURAL CAPITAL AND WRITING

As an alternative to Eagleton's and Berlin's compartmentalized analyses, Pierre Bourdieu's theory of cultural capital offers a forceful model of the complex social and individual forces that drive education in a capitalist economic system. Bourdieu has argued that the accumulation of cultural capital, as it occurs over the course of a lifetime and in the context of its particular historical conditions, can be understood as a process that shapes the social world in two ways: "*Vis instia*, inscribed in objective or subjective structures, but also a *lex instia*—the principle underlying the immanent regularities of the social world—what makes the games of society—not least, the economic game—something other than games of chance" ("Forms" 241). This capital has to be understood in terms of both reproduction and transformation, a process that can be studied historically as what Bourdieu has termed the three forms of cultural capital:

> The embodied state, i.e., in the form of long-lasting dispositions of the mind and body; the objectified state, in the form of the cultural goods (pictures, books, dictionaries, machines, etc.), which are the trace or realization of theories or critiques of those theories, problematics, etc.; and the institutionalized state, a form of objectification which confers entirely original properties on the cultural capital which it is presumed to guarantee. ("Forms" 243)

Bourdieu's ideas outline a descriptive and explanatory methodology in which documents and institutional forms are seen as the "given materials" or "objectified states" of cultural capital, artifacts themselves shaped in terms of the determinations of the contemporaneous economy. What's more, the most profound aims of education in the English language can be understood in terms of the embodied state of cultural capital, the "long-lasting dispositions of the mind and body" as reflected in linguistic skill and sensibility.

Whatever their historical veracity, in this framework Berlin's and Eagleton's conclusions can be understood as a part of a network of professional debates that have helped to shape the specific forms of the cultural capital of English studies. The nationalism emphasized by Eagleton, internalized or not by students, nevertheless helped to shape the canon and so the curriculum and the students' experiences of texts deemed of aesthetic interest. Similarly, the professional status of composition helped to determine the resources at its disposal and so shape its relative successes in educating students. What's more, Bourdieu's work further suggests that this system of cultural capital contributes to the sensibilities and economic lives of professors as well as of students, if not necessarily in identical ways. Importantly, this model can account for the complexity of an education without the reductionism of what Roy Bhaskar terms the stereotypical "illicit identification" models of the relationship between society and the individual (14). What is taught, in other words, need not be what is learned; who we are asked to be need not be who we become.

In this way, we can acknowledge Eagleton's nationalism as well as Berlin's objective ideology as elements in a complex, dynamic process in which the cultural capital of literacy is accumulated. Even more, Bourdieu, while recognizing that the capitalist economy has been in the final analysis always reproduced, also grants to agents a certain degree of autonomy. In the context of my analysis, the capitalism of the 1940s was reproduced (it remained a system based on class and property) as well as transformed (the ramifications of education as a then emerging mass phenomena) through an expansion of access to cultural (and so financial) capital. In brief, the GI Bill allowed hundreds of thousands of soldiers—many of them, including my father, working-class or poor—access to a college education without thereby destroying the fundamental capitalist and democratic principles on which the U.S. economy rests. The close links I have traced out here between the rhetoric of composition, the market, and institutional reform illustrate how change can happen without threatening property relationships. Indeed, in both economic and social terms, wider access to education helped to drive the postwar U.S. economic expansion that reinforced U.S. capitalism. Moreover, while the choices represented in the GI Bill were certainly constrained and shaped by deterministic social and economic forces, the terms of Bourdieu's analysis suggests that individual choice, if not full autonomy, must be taken into account.

In my father's family, for example, only a few men took advantage of the educational opportunities offered as a kind of reward for their wartime service, a decision that would have everything to do with their future social and economic lives. Still, in choosing to get an education, my father entered into an unfamiliar but powerful educational tradition rooted in very dissimilar ideas about the needs of students. In English studies, these traditions had come to be centered on two very different ways of thinking about language. English studies at the university level has historically been divided between what Bourdieu terms a formalist and a popular aesthetic, each governing a separate dimension of literacy. Each, too, carries its own particular pedagogical ideals and methodologies. These closely related educational missions, in effect, add up to a kind of idealized habitus, a set of beliefs and assumptions about what a fully middle-class linguistic sensibility should become through the study of English.

I would argue that literary studies sought to transform the habitus of students through the inculcation of a formalist aesthetic, assuming that students came to college with little exposure to this aesthetic. In contrast, composition's traditional goal was the refinement of a popular ethos that students were assumed to have already acquired, to some degree, through their families and society in general and through the public school system specifically. This popular ethos or aesthetic, however, can be understood only in terms of the formalist aesthetic against which it is defined. Bourdieu's designation is both a matter of the discourses that shaped academic cultural capital and of the institutional arrangements those debates served to justify, reform, or maintain. Neither discipline nor discourse, of course, could have been so successful without the larger socioeconomic forces on which they depended. In particular, the popular ethos that has dominated the teaching of writing characterizes language as a transparent medium through which thought is communicated (more or less accurately, depending on the skill of the writer). Writing is therefore principally judged by ethical and pragmatic, rather than aesthetic, criteria.

The formalist aesthetic that has traditionally underwritten literary studies, in contrast, sees language as problematic, elusive at best and often opaque. Indeed, just as the popular ethos is by definition seen as the non-aesthetic, the formalist aesthetic is by definition seen as the non-useful. The formalist aesthetic, Bourdieu writes in *Distinction*, is explicated most precisely in the work of philosopher Immanuel Kant:

> In contrast to the detachment and disinterestedness which [Kantian] aesthetic theory regards as the only way of recognizing the work of art for what it is, i.e. autonomous, *selbstandig*, the "popular aesthetic" ignores or refuses the refusal of "facile" involvement and "vulgar" enjoyment, a refusal which is the basis of the taste for formal experiment. And popular judgments of paintings or photographs spring from an aesthetic (in fact it is an ethos) which is the exact opposite of the Kantian aesthetic. (4–5)

A "formalist aesthetic," then, can be defined in terms of an "elective distance from the necessities of the natural and social world" and, in the simplest terms, as an inclination to elevate "manner" over "matter" and so "form" over "function" (Bourdieu, *Distinction* 5). The formal properties of language are emphasized along with its communicative function; we look at language as much as we look through it.

What's more, Bourdieu argues, the cultural capital of a formal education is signified by an increasing "stylization of life"; a formal aesthetic is intimately related to schooling. "To be schooled" is in some sense "to be aesthetic." Taste and the relative weight given to a formalist aesthetic serves as a marker of social status, and so as a form of cultural capital, insofar as it signifies a choice no longer wholly dependent on material necessity. In this way, aesthetic taste is linked to financial prosperity. In a formalist aesthetic, for example, a shirt is chosen not simply because it serves its practical function, is inexpensive and well made, and so on but also because it is beautiful or unique. At the formalist extreme of this continuum, a shirt might be chosen precisely because it has little or no practical value. The formalist aesthetic or sensibility is defined in an important sense by way of its opposite: it signifies not poor, potentially even for the poor themselves.

It's important to note that a formalist aesthetic is organized around an epistemology of language and as such cannot be reduced in any simple way to the historical and intellectual phenomenon known as literary formalism. Any notion of language that emphasizes the need for interpretation, "reading between the lines," and the like can be understood as an aesthetics concerned in some sense with "manner" and form. Aesthetic values, in Bourdieu's terms, can serve as markers of class status because to some degree they are dependent on the accumulated cultural capital—the education in both formal and informal senses—of the consumers. In this way, Bourdieu illustrates the close links between patterns of aesthetic values—taste—and the accumulation of social and economic capital. In this context, the value of cultural capital depends on its relative scarcity. Quite literally, fewer people have the surplus time or energy necessary for the accumulation of a distinctly aesthetic sensibility, either with or without the assistance of the school. This has also had a decisive effect on the institutional arrangements of the English department as they are reflected in the professional and disciplinary hierarchies that have shaped the fields of composition and literature.

Bourdieu contends that the status of the formalist aesthetic, which signifies a kind of freedom, is best explained in terms of the historical success of a dominant class and not as an innate capability. "The 'eye,'" Bourdieu writes, "is a product of history reproduced by education" (formal or otherwise), and the hierarchies of the economy have their analogies in the hierarchies of aesthetics:

> To the socially recognized hierarchy of the arts, and within each of them, of genres, schools or periods, corresponds a social hierarchy of the consumers. This predisposes "tastes" to function as markers of class. The manner in which culture has been acquired lives on the manner of using it: the importance attached to manners can be understood once it is seen that it is these imponderables of practice which distinguish the different—and ranked—modes of cultural acquisition, early or late, domestic or scholastic, and the classes of individuals which they characterize. . . . Culture also has its titles of nobility—awarded by the educational system—and its pedigrees,

> measured by seniority in admission to the nobility. (*Distinction* 1)

A habitus, Bourdieu contends, is forged in the compound relationships among social origin and formal and informal education, each of which are themselves shaped by the hierarchies of a class-based, capitalist economy. Again, composition and literary pedagogy sponsored quite different aspects of cultural capital, each in its own way attempting to shape the habitus of students. What is unique to the habitus of the American middle class, at least to the extent that it is represented by the modes of language promulgated by English studies, is the dynamic tension between the accumulation and investment of these inseparable yet very distinct forms of cultural capital.

OBJECTIVITY, PROFESSIONALISM, AND THE MIDDLE-CLASS HABITUS

Importantly, the ethos of my father's writing is consistent with what Hagge has called the "scientific optimism" that first emerged in the late nineteenth and early twentieth centuries:

> Many people felt that social problems could be ameliorated by applying to them the same rational, scientific principles that had allowed engineers—whose achievements were often portrayed in romantic, heroic terms—to span the continent with railway steel, cross mighty chasms with bridges built to be both beautiful and useful, erect towering skyscrapers, and electrify whole cities. ("Early Engineering Textbooks" 439–40)

This "optimism," Hagge says, and the concurrent "ideas of professional literacy and humanistic enculturation" (440) were central to the progressive program advocated by, among others, educational theorist and reformer John Dewey. It was optimistic—and democratic—in that it implied that, with the proper methods, anyone could be taught the scientific knowledge that guided technological and social advances.

Yet these notions of literacy and enculturation, Hagge argues, were by no means completely consensual in either theory or practice, even among their advocates: "In fact, the history of engineering education might be conceptualized as a running battle between those who advocated narrow professional training, and those who wished engineering students to take general humanities courses as well as study a specialized disciplinary curriculum" ("Early Engineering Textbooks" 448). In the terms of my argument, such running battles can be understood as a process or debate shaping the composition of cultural capital as represented in a particular form of university education as well as a specific sort of institution. Within the discipline of English, these struggles are perhaps most dramatically reflected in a division of intellectual labor in which literary studies is associated with the general goals of "humanistic enculturation," while composition is more and more seen in terms of "professional training." This is not to say, of course, that writing instruction, or indeed science, was in any sense "value free"; if this scientific language were to be widely distributed, students would also have to be schooled in a meritocratic value system that would make the labor of education seem a worthwhile investment, both socially and individually.

Indeed, within the field of English, the scientific and technological optimism of an "objective rhetoric" was embedded in what Bloom has called the "middle-class enterprise" of freshman composition. Reviewing a wide range of historians, essayists, and pedagogical theorists, Bloom observes that while socioeconomic class has not historically been an explicit part of the academic discussion of composition pedagogy, "the middle-class pedagogical model . . . has remained normative and dominant from . . . the late nineteenth century to the present" (658). Writing instruction, Bloom argues, has long been centered on a desire to teach students "to think and write in ways that will make them good citizens of the academic (and larger) community, and viable candidates for good jobs upon graduation" (655). These values, Bloom says, include self-reliance, responsibility, and respectability; decorum, propriety, and moderation and temperance; thrift, efficiency, and order; and cleanliness, punctuality, delayed gratification, and critical thinking (655). Freshman composition, Bloom concludes, is designed to eliminate the linguistic and social irregularities young students bring to the university: "Like swimmers passing through the chlorine footbath en route to plunging into the pool, students must first be disinfected in English" (656). My father—and my mother—had to "clean up" a dialect, accent, and syntax that marked them as lower-class and uneducated. What *Unified English Composition* calls the "unwashed necks" of the grammatical forms my parents brought with them from their families could serve all too well as "ambassadors" of their marginal cultural backgrounds; conversely, the objective prose style employed by my father could serve as evidence of his earned professional capabilities. My mother's story of modeling her language style on the educated office workers at the Louisiana capital indicates something of the force of this principle, as does her memory of my father's need for a remedial speech class. These values work on at least two levels: first, as a set of assumptions about language, and second, as formulations of the proper behavior of an educated, middle-class citizen. Social and grammatical propriety are closely related.

The popular ethos is a form of cultural capital that can be used on a daily basis and whose utility appears self-evident. Bourdieu argues that the institutional form of cultural capital itself has a pedagogical effect, contributing substantially to the ongoing evolution of a linguistic sensibility:

> The essential part of what schools communicate is . . . acquired incidentally, such as the system of classification which the school system inculcates through the order in which it inculcates knowledge . . . through the presuppositions of its own organization (the hierarchy of disciplines, sections, exercises etc.) or its operation (mode of assessment, rewards and punishments etc.). (*Distinction* 67)

The institutional divisions of the discipline of English studies, in other words, reinforce and maintain the implicit messages of the intellectual specialization that distinguishes the popular ethos from aesthetics.

Rhetorically, the sequence of courses typical of the U.S. English department suggests that while students may already "know" English, their language must be buffed up before they can go on to more substantive pursuits. Shirley Brice Heath has emphasized, too, that "long before reaching school . . . children have made the transition from home to the larger societal institutions which share the values, skills, and knowledge bases of the school" (368). The linguistic cleansing or polishing of freshman English also reinforces middle-class values; on this foundation rests the enculturation of literary studies. The work of earning cultural capital is framed as a middle-class endeavor in which reward is always already proportional to effort. Similarly, too, professors have traditionally taught writing primarily at the start of their careers, or in graduate school, earning with tenure the right to focus to a greater or lesser extent on literature and research. In each case, privilege is represented as the just reward of hard work in (the English) language.

The accumulation of these values is thus profoundly shaped by economic class long before students enter the classroom; success in admissions, of course, is already indicative of students' ability to adhere to middle-class standards of both taste and labor. Professional success, too, is by definition indicative of the successful internalization of middle-class values. Bloom writes that, for young middle-class Americans, "we . . . scarcely could have found a profession that more thoroughly allowed us to preach what we had been practicing all our lives" (656). Bloom is writing about recent history and, as an established professor of English, is perhaps being a bit too optimistic about the job prospects of young academics. Behind or beneath the veneer of middle-class, hardworking, objective culture often lies a quite different reality. An ideology of merit is in fact as much smoke screen as reality. As many have noted, for example, today more and more institutions rely on adjunct instructors and graduate students in the name of economic efficiency, positions that are in many senses not quite middle-class. David Laurence summarized the situation in "MLA Survey of Staffing in English and Foreign Language Departments, Fall 1999," which documents the increasing use of graduate and adjunct labor in almost 2,000 departments in the United States. "Today," Bill Hendricks has recently written, "most college teachers, whatever their class origins, have working class jobs" (613).

Historically, too, instructors who taught these values were themselves (at least in part) denied many of the ostensible privileges of the professional middle class, including reasonable workloads and the opportunities for professional and financial advancement. Indeed, many would charge that little has changed in this regard. We might also presume that the teaching of these courses, especially to the extent that they were seen as a rite of passage to a literary career, would have some value, however symbolic, as academic capital. In any case, Bloom's description reinforces the often noted point that one of the origins of writing courses lay in a cultural anxiety about the propriety of American English as a feature of a middle-class, and professional, habitus. This anxiety, finally, has to be seen as symptomatic of tensions attendant to the shift from an epoch of social to cultural capital.

How can education, and writing instruction in particular, help to reinforce those values thought necessary to a well-functioning society? In Bloom's view, composition is and will continue to be middle-class because it exists in a kind of closed ideological loop of middle-class teachers instructing middle-class students. More broadly, however, composition is middle-class because it embodies an institutionalized victory, a triumph of the working-class desire for access to cultural as well as financial capital, but at the same time an institutionalization of the middle-class and professional values that have long supported the social compact that enables class mobility in the United States. Composition, however, cannot tell the full story of a linguistic habitus as it is embodied in my father's transcript. To fully understand English studies as cultural capital, we have to examine literary pedagogy as a process through which the university sought to inculcate a formal aesthetic.

3

Literary Studies and the Amateur's "Wow!"

> At all events, there is nothing more universal than the project of objectifying the mental structures associated with the particularity of a social structure. Because it presupposes an epistemological break which is also a social break, a sort of estrangement from the familiar, domestic, native world, the critique (in the Kantian sense) of culture invites each reader, through the "making strange" beloved of the Russian formalists, to reproduce on his or her own behalf the critical break of which it is the product. For this reason it is perhaps the only rational basis for a truly universal culture.
>
> —Pierre Bourdieu, *Distinction*

DAD'S TASTES

IN SEVERAL SENSES, I would call my father's social status as much middle-class in profession as culturally poor or working-class. This hybridity shaped his financial habits as much as his literacy. He never bought a new stereo system, and he owned only a handful of cassettes and old records, largely big band and holiday music; Art Tatum and Bing Crosby were particular favorites, as was Lawrence Welk. Perhaps not surprisingly, this was also likely the sort of music that he had heard in college, or just afterward. He woke up each morning to the same analog clock radio; the family television and record player were always outdated models he had inherited from various relatives or bought from garage sales. Often enough, he got them for little or nothing because they didn't work, and he would repair them so that they functioned well enough for his purposes.

When we were young, he would occasionally take us to the drive-in, but I can otherwise recall him going to see only a handful of movies. He and my mother rarely went out after they began having children, and whenever they did, it was usually to a dinner theater on their anniversary. As their children grew older, my parents did begin to grow interested in a more recognizably middle-class social life, led by my mother, who by now had more free time. She became an avid member of the Toastmasters Club, and my dad would somewhat reluctantly accompany her to various events. At times, I would read her speeches and help her where I could.

My father had converted to Catholicism early in their marriage, ostensibly to please my mother's family and so that they could be married in the church, but he was always a quietly religious man, and he attended Mass every Sunday. His health was never very good; he suffered from what the doctors first called gout, which was rediagnosed toward the end of his life as arthritis. A few years after the belated correction, he died from a heart attack, a condition exacerbated by the large doses of aspirin he took for the often debilitating pain in his hands and knees.

Even in the years before his condition became severe, however, he never owned a pair of tennis shoes or joined a health club. A bicycle was a child's toy, not adult recreation, and, although he flirted with golf in the late 1950s, he never played sports or hunted. He did like to fish and took an avid interest in both my Cub and then Boy Scout troops and in my limited pre-adolescent sports career. My father's notions of gender, while traditional, were also remarkably flexible. He insisted that each of his daughters go to college, even if he envisioned them primarily as future wives and mothers.

In the years before his death, too, as his physical strength declined, he recruited my youngest sister, Jill, to help with working on his car. Women, my dad apparently felt, did not suffer any permanent damage to their femininity by learning to use a mechanic's tools. My mother has said that these lessons in self-reliance surely helped Jill in her difficult struggle to finish college in the years after our father's death. Nevertheless, he clearly was more comfortable with my more masculine childhood activities and left the equivalent feminine interests of my sisters to my mother.

My father's frugality and sense of responsibility never faded, but the older he got, the more economically secure he seemed to feel. I suspect that if he had lived into retirement, he might have found himself more able to experiment with the unfamiliar and the new. Still, I believe that my father felt that he could not explore the freedoms his success represented until he saw his last child finish college. He considered becoming an independent consultant and was convinced he could more than double his income in that way but wanted to wait until he made his twenty years at the city. His sense of responsibility was rooted in sagacity about risk that could have come only from the poverty he knew as a child and from his experiences as a teenager during the war.

This is not to say that my father's adult life was barren or meaningless. He had his wife, his children, and his colleagues, and he took special pleasure in working around the house and in his small workshop full of tools and hardware. One of the perquisites of being a city employee was frequent free tickets to sporting events, and we spent several days a year watching the Colt 45s, and then the Astros, play baseball. It was a particular thrill in the then high-tech Astrodome, completed in 1964.

Dad was a tall, proud man with a lock of jet-black hair that became speckled with gray only in the final years of his life. Until the late 1970s, he continued to wear the same style of heavy, black horn-rimmed glasses he had first purchased twenty years earlier. I wore the same frames until, at age thirteen, I bought wire rims, a style I had seen in pictures of John Lennon. Our extended family admired my father greatly; he was a good provider.

He died in the morning, his favorite time of day, on his beloved orange Naugahyde couch, smoking a pipe over coffee and the newspaper. He had just returned from a trip to Mississippi to see his family and to Louisiana to check up on my sister's new life with her husband, Don. Don had not graduated from high school, and Cynthia had dropped out of college to marry him; Dad was concerned that Cynthia's choice would mean less than the life he had imagined for her. Their trailer home in Sulphur, Louisiana, was modest, but, by all reports, Dad was satisfied. My mother told me she was lying in bed and heard a kind of grunt from my father, and all the commotion of ambulances and emergency medical technicians and hospitals could do nothing for him. He never revived.

Recalling his life from the distance of nearly thirty years, I think my father's cultural and economic practices illustrate that while a college degree allowed him to secure a professional position, it could only start him on the road to (American) middle-class tastes. In important ways, my father lived his life as if he were no better off than he had been as a child. His suspicion of credit, for example, hints at a mistrust of banks and interest that in retrospect seems more appropriate to the poverty of rural Mississippi in the 1930s than to a suburban professional life forty years later. In any case, family obligations always superseded his personal ambition and desire, in the positive sense of individual fulfillment as much as in the potentially negative sense of conspicuous consumption and status seeking. He bought a car, or clothes, primarily for their utilitarian value; he rarely, if ever, made choices according to those fine distinctions of style so common in middle-class consumer culture. A popular ethos, it might be said, rather than a formalist aesthetic anchored his sensibilities.

My father's English-language courses in college reflected a similar division between everyday literacy skills and a more broad-based education in literary taste and knowledge. On the one hand, composition, speech, and technical writing stressed the practical language skills of his professional literacy. Arguably, this form of literacy also dominated the educational values of the early to mid-twentieth century, which emphasized both a popular ethos and individual merit. On the other hand, his literature classes stressed the liberal arts goals of ongoing personal learning and transformation. Again, the history of the U.S. university in the twentieth century suggests that the acquisition of "breeding and social grace," if secondary, was nevertheless an important aspect of what it meant to be an educated American. If the first sort of classes were to give you new abilities, the second suggested the potential of a new way of thinking about the world and, by implication, a new self. Clearly, the former sorts of classes closely meshed with the nominal purposes of his education, as my father understood them—that is, with the accumulation of economic capital. Just as clearly, however, the second sort of courses implied another, closely related set of goals: the accumulation of the tastes and inclinations of a middle-class sensibility, what Pierre Bourdieu has called a habitus.

AESTHETICS AND CLOSE READING AS CULTURAL CAPITAL

In this chapter, I continue my exploration of the traditional composition of the cultural capital of English studies through an examination of Cleanth Brooks and the New Critical School of literary criticism. For many, Brooks is the exemplary New Critic, epitomizing an era of political oversimplification and cultural denial. Our contemporary concern with class, race, and gender is portrayed as a decisive and necessary reversal of his sort of thinking, a return to a more complex, historically based literary theory. In recent years, however, this congratulatory vision of the New Critics and Brooks has begun to shift in favor of a more nuanced narrative. Even in these newer critiques, however, New Criticism is most often defined as a movement more interested in theory than in students. My aim here is to supplement this emerging view of literary history and the New Critics with a reading of Brooks's work as a pedagogy centered on the inculcation of a formalist aesthetic. Here, too, I hope to weaken the influence of those disciplinary studies that have traditionally created quite separate historical visions of composition and literary studies. Each, in my view, contributes to the larger aims of English studies as a methodology of class mobility and as the inculcation of a habitus.

To this end, I pay special attention to Brooks's views of language and history, views that I believe are better explained as pedagogy than as ideology. Far from denying history, I argue that Brooks's conception of literary education in the university is founded on a direct confrontation with socioeconomic class in general and class mobility in particular. Indeed, to the extent that the English studies classroom continues to rely on close reading, this engagement remains central to the goals that have long undergirded the liberal arts as well as English studies. I begin with Brooks's observation that literary instruction must contend with what he terms the "pressures towards direct statement" rooted in both his students' education and in society at large ("Forty Years" 6). This pressure, I contend, has its roots in the historical circumstances in which Brooks taught.

Relying on a variety of texts written by Brooks over his long career, I show that, in Bourdieu's terms, Brooks saw his students' assumptions about language as founded in a resilient popular ethos. Literary instruction, in Brooks's view, represents an attempt to accomplish the difficult task of changing an epistemology of language and communication that seems everywhere confirmed by common sense. His work was successful, Brooks contends, only to the extent that it aided teachers in their attempts to transform students' assumptions about language. In this sense, Brooks's pedagogy was designed as a sophisticated counterweight to the rise of objective, scientific epistemology. Brooks attempted to position skepticism and contemplation alongside the rhetorics of objectivity and merit that were so successfully transforming U.S. society.

In this view, Brooks's work centers not so much on the construction of a literary theory or canon as on the inculcation of a formalist aesthetic. Theory should serve pedagogy rather than vice versa. Brooks's ambition was to create what might be called a countertaste, a habitus that views language as problematic and ambiguous. Drawing on the work of John Guillory, I finish this chapter with a discussion of the contemporary relevance of Brooks's pedagogical aims. As has often been noted, in an age so dedicated to vocation, literary studies seems to have lost its relevance. Even if we reject the literary theories of the New Critics, I contend, their attempt to ensure the widest possible distribution of this form of cultural capital is worth emulating. Clearly, in our time as well as Brooks's, we need an educational counterweight to objective certainty.

CLEANTH BROOKS AND THE TRIUMPH OF THE NEW CRITICISM

It is difficult to document in a precise way the classroom methodologies of the late 1940s, literary or otherwise. Nevertheless, it seems safe to assume that the work of Cleanth Brooks, who taught at LSU from 1932 to 1947, decisively shaped my father's education in the English language. Brooks, Mark Royden Winchell writes, "was probably the most important literary critic to come to prominence during the second third of the twentieth century" (xi). Gerald Graff, John Guillory says, "observes that by the time Cleanth Brooks publishes *The Well Wrought Urn* (1947), it is no longer necessary for the New Critics to polemicize further" (157). The transformation of criticism, with its pedagogy of close reading, was launched by an entire generation of critics and had arguably occurred even before my father reached LSU.

What's more, in the decade before my father attended college, Brooks's ideas had surely met an audience already well-versed in the pedagogical problems on which they were based, difficulties associated with the changing demographics of students. Whatever a teacher's position on literary theory, in other words, literary academics shared a common pedagogical dilemma. Along with Brooks, the LSU faculty of the 1930s and 1940s also included such New Critical popularizers as Thomas Austin Kirby, then chair of the English department, and William Van O'Connor.

While Cleanth Brooks is today perhaps most often thought of as a literary theorist, his equally important career as a textbook author began much earlier with *An Approach to Literature*, written by Brooks, Robert Penn Warren, and John Thibaut Purser, first published in the fall of 1936 by F. S. Crofts and Company. And in 1938, Brooks and Warren published *Understanding Poetry*, a book, Winchell notes, "that would revolutionize the teaching of literature for more than a generation" (156). Yet Brooks's pedagogical notions have most often been downplayed in favor of his powerful influence on the discipline of literary studies and of his status as one of the founding fathers of the New Criticism.

Despite Brooks's own contentions, the critical ideas of New Criticism, rather than its pedagogical methodology, are often seen as his most significant legacy. Brooks's account of New Criticism is, in important ways, consistent with a newer view of the history of literary criticism and education in the United States. Indeed, Brooks's notions of the "literariness" of history can sound remarkably contemporary. It is important to note that in "Forty Years of Understanding Poetry," Brooks defined the crucial debate over criticism in terms of classroom methods in particular and not necessarily in terms of the "newfangled" ideas of his literary theory. Brooks's summary of his project is worth quoting:

> What were our intentions for the book [*Understanding Poetry*]? Did we expect to sweep the field? Certainly not. I remember a conversation in which we agreed that we would be satisfied if we could interest as much as twenty percent of the profession. . . . [W]e were avowedly innovating[,] . . . upsetting time honored methods. The first really encouraging hint came in 1939 when the CEA [College English Association], in conjunction with the MLA, held its annual convention in New Orleans. I . . . found myself at the banquet sitting next to William Clyde Devane, then Dean of Yale College. I was completely surprised when he told me that *Understanding Poetry* had been adopted for a remodeled freshman English course. The younger men in the department had staged . . . something like a mild palace revolution. (7)

For Brooks, the innovation of his method wasn't so much in which texts were to be included in any proposed canon or course or in an institutional need for professional legitimacy (although to be successful he certainly needed legitimacy) but in "upsetting time honored methods" of literary *instruction*. University professors, Brooks submits, eventually embraced his textbook, not so much because it helped them to achieve a certain measure of intellectual status but because it met the perceived pedagogical needs of the younger professors who, then as now, were most likely to be involved in the teaching of low-level literary courses.

Brooks also contends that the origins of his notions lay in his experiences as a young professor and in his colleagues' attempts to succeed at their jobs. It's not often noted that Brooks himself spent many years as an adjunct professor.

> I got my first job at LSU in 1932 and [Robert Penn] Warren joined me there in 1934. He said he was fired from Vanderbilt. It was difficult during the depression to get any sort of work. My friends and I, there were about a dozen of us in all, enjoyed reading literature, especially poetry, and we were discovering new ways of reading it freshly, and perhaps more powerfully, and sharing this with other people. (Spurlin, Fisher, and Brooks 371)

Evan Carton and Gerald Graff argue that historical accounts of the predominance of New Critical literary thought in the decades after the 1930s, with their emphasis on consensus, obscure the other possible "criticisms" with which New Criticism historically contended. This intellectual obscurantism is analogous to a more general social obscurantism that has shrouded Brooks's pedagogical ambitions.

For Brooks, this contentious process was a struggle between generations of university instructors over differing conceptions of pedagogical methods and not solely or necessarily between intrinsic and extrinsic criticisms. It was a struggle that, of course, occurred within an academic pecking order, and part of Brooks's difficulty was that he was not a full professor, with the appropriate authority for his argument. Worse, at least at first, he was a textbook writer. Brooks's originating impetus was the "serious practical problem" of teaching literature rather than ideas about the discipline of literary criticism as such ("Forty Years" 5). Brooks believed his methodology addressed the problems associated with the transmission of a literary sensibility, not criticism per se, which must necessarily contain elements of both literary and non-literary explication. In addition, importantly, Brooks argued that a more or less simple recital of the historical and biographical facts relevant to any particular text cannot support the inculcation of a formalist aesthetic.

In an essay published in the *CEA NewsLetter* in 1940, Brooks responds to what he felt was the mistaken idea that literary studies seeks to do no more than expose students to literature:

> Can literature be taught? Miss Willa Cather, in our last *NewsLetter*[,] says that it cannot be "'taught' in the sense that Latin

> can be taught," and that by inference she asks for little more than that the student be "exposed" to the classics of literature in hopes that the student may be infected. . . . Obviously, literature cannot be taught as Latin can be, but I think it might be taught nearly as well as football is taught. . . . In both cases native ability will vary greatly from student to student, but good coaching is indispensable; and in both cases, a self-discipline must be acquired in action. ("What Are English Teachers Teaching?" 3)

Brooks reminds us that, whatever the particular literary or theoretical inclinations of his or any other generation, university instructors must still contend with the difficulties of teaching an aesthetic sensibility. Students may or may not have talent, but with the help of a good coach, they can learn "in action" the self-discipline of close reading. *Understanding Poetry* was successful, Brooks argues, not solely or simply because it helped to shape an academically legitimate discourse but because it met the practical needs of classroom instruction. Whatever the state of the discipline, Brooks believed literary instruction must always be concerned with pedagogy and with the broader social situation in which literary education occurs.

Brooks himself, while acknowledging the contention engendered by the "mild palace revolution" of his book's acceptance, emphasized not so much the national identity of his students as their common sensibilities rooted in a popular aesthetic or ethos. Brooks, echoing Bourdieu, defined this pedagogical task not in terms of native intelligence but as a problem of competing sensibilities. Recalling the genesis of *Understanding Poetry* in his classrooms at LSU in the 1930s and 1940s, Brooks writes:

> Our students were not stupid. They were simply, if I may use a theological term, almost "invincibly ignorant." Nobody had ever tried to take them inside a poem or a story, or tried to explain how a poem worked, or, if I may borrow a phrase from Emily Dickinson, no one had shown them how a poem, in telling the truth, has to tell it *slant*. For all our students' previous reading and instruction had stressed one virtue only.

> The purpose of all discourse was to convey information and to deliver it straight. ("Forty Years" 6; emphasis in original)

Looking back over his career four decades after the publication of his influential textbook, Brooks stresses not so much the theoretical importance of his work—"our dominant motive was not to implant newfangled ideas in the innocent Louisiana sophomores we faced three times a week" ("Forty Years" 6)—but its pedagogical efficacy. Literary instruction, Brooks believed, had to be conducted in the face of an already existing aesthetic or ethos—it sought to transform this popular aesthetic ("to convey information and to deliver it straight") into a formalist aesthetic ("a poem, in telling the truth, has to tell it *slant*").

This project, Brooks notes, met with only minimal success, if that success is measured in strictly literary terms: "I can't boast that I was successful in teaching the poem. Who ever is, for that matter?" ("Forty Years" 6). To some extent, this sense of failure can be explained in terms of Brooks's contention that the literary experience is never finished and so is ephemeral, that is, beyond any simple representation in language or pedagogical methodology. Consequently, Brooks says, you may never feel that you have completely succeeded in expressing your own experience, literary or otherwise. Yet, Brooks claims, he did succeed in creating a kind of shared aesthetic framework:

> The students and I could thenceforward at least talk about the basic themes of the "Rape of the Lock," and about its structure, and we had laid a basis for talking about the poet's very complicated attitude towards Belinda, and why he devises his metaphors, allusions, and even his metrical patterns in order to define and develop his attitude toward her and toward society at large. ("Forty Years" 7)

This is not to say, of course, that Brooks believed that his students already and fully knew how to "deliver it straight." The popular ethos students brought with them, he suggests, was more a matter of inclination and professed value than specific skill: "Alas, the prose that our students themselves wrote was scarcely a model of lucidity. In fact, the pressures towards direct statement had succeeded in killing their aptitude for poetry without teaching them how to write decent expository prose" ("Forty Years" 6). Brooks argues that these "pressures towards direct statement," what Bourdieu would call a naive involvement in texts, has its roots not just in the previous education and social background of the students but in the everyday reading habits encouraged by the culture at large. Literary pedagogy must fight an uphill battle, Brooks believed, against the inefficacy of experience and the linguistic epistemology of the popular ethos. In more modern literary terms, each in its way tends to collapse text into book.

LITERARY PEDAGOGY, CLASS, AND THE TRANSFORMATION OF SENSIBILITY

To make use of Bourdieu's terms, literacy is defined in Brooks's work as governed by a kind of commonsensical ethos or aesthetic of communication that, among other things, admits no distinction among cultural arenas or domains. Brooks believed that his students needed to learn to "'differentiate' and 'appreciate' the formal qualities that distinguish genres of discourse." Describing his students, Brooks emphasizes the popular ethos they brought to the literary experience of reading: "Many of them approached a Shakespeare sonnet or Pope's 'Rape of the Lock' as they would approach an ad in a Sears Roebuck Catalogue or an editorial in their local newspaper. For example, one of [Robert Penn] Warren's students, to whom he was teaching *King Lear*, would mournfully shake her head and mutter: 'I just don't like to read about bad people'" ("Forty Years" 5). Brooks argues that his methodology is shaped first of all by an attempt to overcome his students' inclination to reject the "primacy of form over function" (Bourdieu, *Distinction* 5). A sensibility that saw only the "bad people" of Shakespearean drama would, ideally, learn to recognize and differentiate among the formalist, aesthetic elements that marked, for example, an Elizabethan text as dissimilar to a newspaper (Brooks, "Forty Years" 5).

My father's story supports Brooks's proposition that a transformation of taste or aesthetic sensibility can be understood only within the complex dynamics of educational and social background. Brooks suggests that students of the time brought to the classroom an aesthetic or ethos of reading and writing that seemed especially resistant to the inculcation of a formalist literary aesthetic. In Bourdieu's terms, students had to learn to "believe in the representation" (*Distinction* 5) rather than in the things represented, to evaluate a specifically literary, formalist art of characterization, for example, rather than to simply pass judgment on the ethics or morality of the person represented.

The pedagogy of the New Criticism, as represented by Brooks, attempted to teach students to read against the grain of a culture in which science was considered both more important and more democratic. Brooks's goal was to teach his students to see the language itself, not simply to look through the text to the world or idea it sought to present. Arguably, if a teacher is successful in inculcating a literary epistemology, students might also begin to see the language of the newspaper in terms of the problematic of language rather than as simple knowledge or information passing through a transparent medium. The ability to recognize and evaluate formal properties of literature, Bourdieu suggests, is important because it is at least potentially "transposed" into the ability to identify and evaluate formalist properties as such. It provides, in Brooks's phrase, a slant, a kind of framework for the appreciation and evaluation of cultural choices generally. Literary evaluation in this sense becomes a model, say, for the evaluation of a television series or of the poetic beauty of a shirt. This "stylization" of life can then, insofar as it signifies an "active distance from necessity," serve as a marker of social status (Bourdieu, *Distinction* 5).

More important, for Brooks, the aesthetics of writing can affect life more generally because it influences thinking as such and so the writer's view of self, language, and world. Brooks contended that all writing—even expository writing—ought to contribute to a life-long process of self-transformation and revelation. Because language and aesthetics are open-ended, knowledge loses some of the certainty that is an implicit danger of objective epistemology and science. In this sense, Brooks's pedagogical philosophy emphasizes that a certain linguistic epistemology, a way of understanding language, rather than a canon of great works or a closed definition of literature as such, ought to govern literary pedagogy. His contention, again, is not metaphysical but social: we need people, Brooks might have said, who are skeptical about language and objectivity. This linguistic skepticism, Brooks believed, ought to be at the heart of what Bourdieu would call a middle-class habitus. In Brooks and Warren's composition textbook, *Modern Rhetoric*, first published in 1949, the authors argue that good writing demands self-reflection; rote learning is explicitly rejected in favor of an ongoing process of discovery:

> Good writing cannot be learned—or cannot readily be learned—by a process of blind absorption, trial and error, or automatic conditioning. It is learned as the student becomes aware of the underlying principles. If, in the practical day-to-day business of writing, the student can be made to be constantly aware of the principles underlying what he is trying to do, then he comes to a deeper realization of the workings of his own mind and feelings and, through that realization, to a greater skill in expressing himself. (ix)

Expository writing, Brooks and Warren contend, is important, "first as a means of communication, and second as a means of thinking" (6). In addition, if learning to write is at the same time a process of learning how to think, then language empowers by allowing the student to think (see) the world more clearly. "Lacking competence in language," the authors warn students, "you will spend much of your life fumbling in a kind of twilight in which facts and ideas are perceived only dimly and often in distorted shapes" (4).

Modern Rhetoric, however, unlike *Unified English Composition* or current-traditional rhetoric generally, is not concerned solely with language as a transparent medium of communication. Here, as well as in literature, writing involves an understanding of the formal properties of language and of the impact of context on the writer's aesthetic choices:

> As an instrument for expressing emotion, language necessarily undertakes to discriminate shades of feeling. The poet's metaphor and the schoolboy's bit of slang have this purpose in common—and the bit of slang sometimes serves the purpose better than the metaphor. At this point we cannot go into a

> discussion of the various means which language employs to make these discriminations . . . but we can emphasize the fact that in discriminating shades of feeling, language helps us to understand our emotions and to understand ourselves. (8)

Writing, then, represented to Brooks a way of learning to think and to see and so to understand formally, aesthetically, and ethically. The indistinct shapes of the world could through this writing become both clear and beautiful. In contrast to *UEC*, Brooks's formulation is ethos *and* aesthetics, not ethos *over* aesthetics.

It seems reasonable to assume that my father's lack of previous education made the inculcation of this sensibility difficult at best. As a whole, the education system would simply not have believed it economically viable to spend the time and energy needed to successfully confront an epistemology that so many other interests supported so fully. Economic rationalization put limits on progressive ideology; capitalism curbed democratic impulses. Indeed, in many senses, Brooks's linguistic skepticism can be read as a corrective to the naive faith of the progressive, liberal arts agenda that drove the rapid expansion of the university system in the first three decades of the twentieth century. In any case, the academic triumph of New Critical literary education in the English department had strict limits clearly marked out in my father's transcript. Yet my father's stories to me do imply that this formalist aesthetic could also survive as a kind of educational and existential ideal, if one that could be achieved only given either an appropriate "social pedigree" or, again, the willingness, on the part of students as well as institutions, to invest the time and energy required. Indeed, insofar as Brooks saw the literary as ineffable, always already just out of reach of full articulation, he too defined it as an ideal rather than as a pragmatic goal.

Professionally, my father would likely have not been particularly well served by an ability to talk about what were then considered to be the most important—however defined—literary texts and authors of his day. It seems unlikely that canonical knowledge as such had much if anything to do with his desires for his children's education. Yet, at least potentially, the view of language on which literary studies rests might well have assisted him in his reading and writing. Indeed, it was this view, as well as the focus on aesthetic transformation, that I would argue constitutes the lasting legacy of the New Criticism. It might be too much to ask that any member of the middle class carefully consider the formal properties of every piece of quotidian writing he or she produces. Nonetheless, the ability to see language in this way is clearly consonant with a middle-class sensibility more generally, at least as represented by traditional American educational values. Skepticism about the certainties of science and the claims of experts is as important to a democracy now as it was a half century ago. In strict economic terms, of course, a manager would likely prefer his or her employees to remain compliant and credulous.

Brooks's late-1970s defense of his methods, published when New Criticism was under fire from all sides, might be seen as disingenuous and as downplaying what he calls the "newfangled" ideas he and his like-minded contemporaries introduced into literary studies. Certainly, under the regime of the apprentice system, Brooks mistakenly saw little reason to question the structure of the English department or to examine the economic foundation of the status his methodologies helped literary professors accumulate. Yet Brooks's pedagogy, and particularly his handling of history, is more complex than the traditional view of his work might suggest. Brooks, moreover, argued throughout his career that while history has a place in the literary classroom, it must be put into a specifically pedagogical context. Again, even history, as a form of writing, cannot be understood or taught without reference to the epistemology of a formalist aesthetic. The New Critics were accused of advocating a methodology that could be used to present, if not promote, a view of literature as radically divorced from the contingencies of its social origins. Brooks argues, however, that the graduate education of college instructors—rooted in historical, linguistic, and biographical scholarship—made this literary reductionism unlikely at best. While many have contended that the New Criticism has downplayed history, the research supporting such a claim has been almost completely disciplinary rather than pedagogical.

Brooks, comparing his own literary textbook to others of the time, argues that the ahistoricism his criticism is often accused of is factually inaccurate. His focus on literary techniques, Brooks contends, only served to supplement the methodology of teachers and critics already well versed in the biographical and historical contexts of literature. Brooks, in other words, implicitly recognized the importance of the distribution of labor in the U.S. university and of curricular sequence; graduate students, he knew, while often teaching composition, are taught by professors who provide extensive historical background. Graduate school education, however, presumes a quite different constituency than does undergraduate English. In effect, then, Brooks is arguing that what is efficacious for graduate students and professors is not necessarily efficacious for undergraduates. History is set aside, but the impulse is curricular and developmental rather than foundational and disciplinary. In this view, students, having taken literary classes, would then approach their other subjects quite differently, recognizing that in each subject they would find the same problematic of knowledge and language.

THE PLACE OF HISTORY

For Brooks, what was "new" about the New Criticism was not its reduction of the text to a purified literary object but its addition of a systematic formalist methodology to the repertoire of criticism and instruction. As a teacher, he believed that this methodology ought to be the starting point for education generally. Literature came first, pedagogically speaking, because all texts, even historical texts, were shaped by the epistemology implied in a formalist aesthetic. A student who learned history—even literary history—before these lessons in epistemology might well mistake argument for truth. Brooks, in short, believed that a teacher trained only in historical or biographical exegesis was ill prepared to face the difficult task of attempting to transform the linguistic sensibilities students brought to the classroom. Arguably, this was a particularly acute problem in the middle decades of the twentieth century, which saw a rapid rise in college enrollment of working-class students relatively less exposed to formal education. And, of course, one of the most significant of these growth spurts in admissions occurred at the very moment of New Criticism's triumph, the period just after World War II.

For Brooks, the aim of the transformation was, at bottom, the aim of progressive, democratic education: the cultivation of skepticism in a culture everywhere promoting credulity. Historically, it must be remembered, Brooks's work happened against the background of both fascism and the rapid scientific and technological change that accompanied the war. In *Understanding Drama*, for example, first published in 1945 with Robert B. Heilman, the authors emphasize that literary history, while important, must be seen in specific relation to the literary form in question:

> We have remarked that the first consideration of this manual has been the problem of reading drama with appreciation and understanding. But the editors do not intend to discredit the claims of literary history. Much of the historical material, of course, will be provided by the teacher, and the teachers will wish to supplement this manual with readings in the story of the drama. Teachers who wish to stress the historical approach will find a succinct history of the drama in Appendix B. (xi)

Again, the pedagogical sequence is important in this context: Brooks contends that before one can understand literature in or as history, one first has to comprehend a formalist aesthetic and epistemology.

Even more, this aesthetic awareness must be approached in gradual steps, "from rather simple problems to increasingly complex ones" (ix). The structure of the book, then, represents not an essentialist view of history but a pragmatic pedagogical strategy. Literally, for the young undergraduate student, history is presented as an appendix to the book of representative dramatic forms, whose central aim is to assist the teacher in his or her attempt to teach certain aspects of a formalist aesthetic, here in the context of the drama. Closing the circle, the student is then implicitly invited to read history itself in terms of a formalist aesthetic, as a form of writing as dependent on so-called literary devices as any other. In Brooks's hands, the New Criticism sought to supplement rather than to replace the biographical and historical criticism he believed was already well represented in the training of professors.

The importance of his method, Brooks contends, was its focus on the transformation of the aesthetic sensibilities of students rather than on any particular notion of literature. In Brooks's view, the ostensible dangers of his approach were outweighed by the value of an epistemology of language that could undermine or transform the certainties of the popular ethos. Brooks's ideas suggest that the early success and longevity of the New Criticism was due in large part to its focus on addressing the difficult problem of educating students into an epistemology that contradicted the way of using language that students everywhere encountered. Even professors who lamented the ahistorical, formalist bent of New Criticism shared the sociological and pedagogical dilemmas that drove its creation. For Brooks, whatever the concerns of the "disciplinary" debates, his methodology was persuasive because it met a pedagogical need shared by anyone who sought to teach the formalist aesthetic that underlies non-utilitarian language. The degree of difficulty of this task, of course, can be described in terms of socioeconomic class and the accumulation of literacy and cultural capital.

The ambiguities of literature, in brief, were to counter the apparent certainties of science. The politics of the New Critics, Wallace W. Douglas wrote in 1962 (quoting William K. Wimsatt Jr., one of Brooks's textbook collaborators), were not particularly subtle: "A very simple content analysis will prove that their poetic theory, even though it is notorious for defending the integrity of the poem as an organic unity, could give one of the biggest pushes, perhaps . . . the biggest, to the mid-century American 'religo-aesthetic reaction' against progressive 'liberalism' and 'scientism'" (2). Again, Brooks's description of the origins and success of his textbooks also emphasizes this notion of "competing" sensibilities in the context of the university classroom. Yet for Brooks, the politics involved were, in essence, the politics of class mobility. In such an environment, too, the politics of literature must be pedagogical as well as disciplinary.

This reading of Brooks's work suggests that the debate over literature and its apparent irrelevance has to be understood as an ongoing historical struggle against a perceived danger inherent in objectivity rather than as a specific definition of literature. Ironically, in this sense, literature shares composition's more often noted problem of legitimacy. Our investment in the teaching of literature no longer seems justifiable, Guillory has recently argued, because the perceived socioeconomic needs for cultural capital have changed. Guillory sees this shift in cultural capital as one away from literature and toward composition.

> The crisis of the literary syllabus is that it is indeed no longer the basis of the vernacular standard. This is one reason that the literary syllabus should seem to us now so vulnerable to the charge of a failure to "represent" various social groups, while the syllabus of composition proceeds quietly with the work of producing a language that is at once manifestly privileged, and which aspires to "universality," the same claim that was once asserted virtually without dissent for the literary curriculum. (81)

Yet, this debate focuses, for Guillory, not on a historical understanding of literature and its distribution but on the canon. Literary study, Guillory concludes, has not developed a persuasive social rationale based on its historical purposes and its potential place in a capitalist economy. A familiarity with canonical texts, in other words, no longer serves as an effective status marker, if it ever did. Similarly, literary writing no longer serves as the "gold standard" for language as such; to be literate increasingly means to communicate effectively rather than in an aesthetically pleasing or interesting manner. Put another way, the contemporary economy rewards articulate communication more than artistic sensibility, clarity more than wit, utility over beauty. As I have argued in my reading of *UEC*, however, in this formulation aesthetics is subordinated rather than dismissed.

Guillory focuses his study on what in this context can be called an investigation of the disciplinary debate over aesthetics as it has occurred in intellectual history, generally speaking. In particular, Guillory shows that the historical roots of aesthetic discourse lie in an attempt to create a non-utilitarian realm distinct from (economic) exchange values. The most important effect of this opposition, he concludes, is a compartmentalization of literary art in "the discourse of canonicity . . . the illusion that aesthetic experience is really restricted to the experience of High Cultural Works" (336). Here echoing Susan Miller, Guillory argues that in rejecting the "low" of the marketplace, the discipline of literature has seemingly become convinced that aesthetics is a separate realm altogether. In seeking legitimacy, then, the discipline of literary studies has become mired in a search for a representative canon rather than in a critique of the means of production and consumption of literacy. Such a critique, Guillory says, would focus on reform of the "grotesquely unequal" distribution of cultural capital through the education system rather than on a debate of the merits of various texts, aesthetic or otherwise. This is an inequity, I would argue, well represented by my father's experiences.

Drawing on what he calls Bourdieu's more utopian ideas, Guillory attempts to articulate an alternative to aesthetics as usual:

> Bourdieu knows that some autonomy (relative autonomy) is the condition for the appropriation of the products of the cultural producers by the moneyed class; otherwise such products would have no "value," no status as cultural capital for the dominant classes who appropriate them. Nevertheless, the struggle for autonomy is worth waging, on behalf of a "republic of artists and intellectuals," a domain in which the principle of restricted production is universalized. (339)

Rejecting the notion that aesthetics and commerce are diametrically opposed, Guillory claims, does not mean we must also reject our "relative autonomy" as intellectuals and teachers. Guillory is not arguing that the university should become no more than a training ground for professionals, or that a new hegemony of utility be embraced. Neither, however, can we simply choose to reject the popular ethos as irrelevant to our project of creating a "republic of artists and intellectuals"; absolute autonomy is politically naive at best. As I have argued here, communicative efficacy and art are both worthy social (and individual) goals. Instead, Guillory says, the crisis in literature has to be met in a disciplinary focus on the various ways that literacy is shaped and maintained in our culture and in an ongoing attempt to make access to education universal.

As Brooks might say, the question is not what is literature, and so what texts are more representative of our aesthetic ideals, but how can we teach a formalist aesthetic given the economic force of the popular ethos. We need changes in how we think about literature, in other words, but we also need changes in the institutions in which we work.

Clearly, then, a reappraisal of Cleanth Brooks needs to proceed within a new understanding of the complexity of the debate that surrounded the institutionalization of his pedagogical methods as much as his disciplinary ideals. Brooks's work, like *UEC*, has to be read as a technology of class mobility and as an attempt to articulate how teaching can help to ensure the widest availability of cultural capital. If we believe, in other words, that the task of literary instruction is still important, we must begin to understand how we might facilitate the inculcation of the formalist aesthetic and epistemology, whatever canon or canons are said to be paramount, and whatever conceptual model we choose to adopt as our theoretical and pedagogical framework. At the heart of this understanding has to be a reversal of our traditional institutional understanding in which the popular ethos is seen in terms of an ongoing, productive dialectic with a formal aesthetic. If ethos needs utopia, art also needs pragmatism.

Guillory contends that current debates must move away from notions of representation in the canon and toward an understanding of the place and purposes of a specifically literary form of cultural capital. This new debate, I would argue, would be both utopian in its desire to create a new and better world and hard-nosed in its focus on pedagogy and institutions. Even in the context of the United States, a formal aesthetics of writing as an epistemology of language still has social and economic efficacy, even if canonical knowledge does not. In Guillory's terms, aesthetics and exchange are deeply intertwined in a common social history. Without a pedagogy of the formalist aesthetic, I would contend, English studies educators can only compound the fiscal inequities of socioeconomic class with an equally important cultural divide between aesthetic and epistemological haves and have-nots.

THE DISCIPLINE OF ENGLISH STUDIES AND THE FORMALIST AESTHETIC

In considering a pedagogy of the formalist aesthetic, it is helpful to recall Mike Rose's depiction of academic socialization. Rose contends that graduate training reinforces a sharp division between what he calls "the preservation of a discipline" and the "intellectual development of young minds" (194). The former, Rose says, is significantly different in focus from the latter:

> Graduate training forces you to give a tremendous amount of thought to the development of your discipline, to its methods, exemplary studies, and central texts. People emerge from graduate studies, then, as political scientists or botanists, but not as educators. That is, though professors may like to teach . . . it is pretty unlikely that they have been encouraged to think about, say, the cognitive difficulties young people have . . . as they learn to conduct inquiry . . . [or] the reading or writing difficulties that attend the development of . . . reasoning. (196)

Not surprisingly, Rose implies, the accentuation of disciplinary investigation over pedagogy leaves many professors ill prepared for the students they will meet in their classrooms. Consequently, Rose notes, recalling Terry Eagleton's notion of the guardians, professors too often see their pedagogical task as centered in "monitoring the rightness or wrongness of incursions into [their] discipline" (197). Rose also emphasizes that these scholars are therefore too often unskilled at understanding learning or at tracking its progress.

This separation of pedagogy from research also served as a founding principle of the most prestigious sectors of the modern U.S. university system as it evolved out of its English and German influences. In addition, as Rose notes, "these issues [of pedagogy], if addressed at all in the academy, are addressed in schools of education, and most faculty hold schools of education in low regard" (196). Rose's division, I would argue, can also be used to describe much current historical scholarship on literary studies in general and on New Criticism in particular. Perhaps not surprisingly, even those inquiries that focus on pedagogy seem more interested in the "discipline" than in the "intellectual development of young minds."

The concerns of English studies, too often, are less representative of the aspirations of students than of their professors. Typical of this focus on the discipline is our contemporary view of Cleanth Brooks. This focus on the discipline and its guardians has helped to obscure Brooks's belief that any effort to inculcate a formalist aesthetic is at the same time a projected transformation of the popular ethos. In his pedagogy, Brooks was seeking not so much to raise young literary scholars, as is often implicitly argued, but to transform the sensibilities of students destined for professional careers. Brooks's influential pedagogy did not seek to create a literary elite but to propagate an epistemological counterweight to scientific objectivity. Rose's comments also hint at the impact of objective evaluation and scientism within the realm of literary instruction; Brooks felt compelled to describe literary knowledge as a separate but equal form of learning. A democratic society, Brooks believed, needed its literary experiences as much as its scientific knowledge.

The sequence of course work in English studies is especially important in this context: first the student's ethos of writing is refined, and only then is there an attempt to supplement ethos with a nuanced formal aesthetic. It is this hierarchy, aesthetic over ethos, that needs to be challenged. Importantly, Brooks also suggests that before the graduate student can begin to comprehend the varieties of literary discourse, the undergraduate must understand the formalist aesthetic as such. Brooks, I believe, correctly recognized (if without precisely articulating) the difficulty as well as the social, economic, and political importance of a formalist aesthetic in a culture dominated by both scientism and the hierarchies of a capitalist economy. The political impulses of agrarian ideology evolved, in short, into a complex but sharply focused populist project. At the heart of this agenda was a belief that aesthetic knowledge could arm students against what was seen as a dehumanizing industrial system. Yet Brooks's ambition may seem—indeed, has been seen as—naive at best and dangerously distorting at worst, and almost from its birth, New Criticism has been attacked for its so-called historical elisions.

In an interview conducted with William J. Spurlin and Michael Fisher just before his death in 1992, Brooks contends that the "universality" of literature cannot be seen as a conclusion of criticism but as a kind of hypothesis, a question that arises out of the process of teaching close reading:

> You are right, I think, that the term "universal" might be loaded culturally, socially, and we have to use these terms loosely. Regarding your point about certain ideas being put across to students as universal, I think we need to get back to the idea of critical pedagogy. Once again, I think teachers tend to simplify in the classroom because they are in search of that well-oiled machine that the New Criticism or any other method of reading simply cannot provide. We have to help students get really close to a text, to help them find something over which to ponder. (380)

The idea of New Critical reductionism, Brooks thought, arose from a mistaken notion that as a "well-oiled machine," it sought to predecide the reading experience for the student.

New Critical tenets, Brooks argues, including universality, are works-in-progress rather than facts, and it is the desire for determinate meaning that largely explains the ongoing misconceptions about what he was trying to accomplish:

> There is a risk to "anything goes" if we believe we can abandon altogether the text, history, and so on. Our technocratic world emphasizes means and how to get things done. We tend to think that we know what we want and that it is just a matter of getting there; hence, the well-oiled machine of which I used to speak of the reception and use of the New Criticism earlier. But with this said . . . I believe that while we cannot discount the role of the text in reading, the text is not some kind of sanctified object outside of any relation to the world. That would be silly. What I'm trying to say is that we need to take the text seriously to avoid this "anything goes" you mention, and then ask what responses are possible. We need to work hard, and real hard. (Spurlin, Fisher, and Brooks 378)

In Brooks's view, the indeterminacy of language suggests not so much that a text can mean anything a reader might desire but that interpretations are always rooted in debate and judgments of plausibility. Interpretation is a process of persuasion about texts, and to a greater or lesser extent, evidence for any textual interpretation has to come, in the end, from those texts.

New Critical literary notions, Brooks says, placed history into a specifically literary context: "History means a story, it is a narrative, a text: it isn't necessarily claiming to be the truth. Some people may claim that history is true in an absolutist sense, but I don't think that is what history has ever tried to claim" (Spurlin, Fisher, and Brooks 369). Here the literary and the historical stand in for an epistemology, a way of understanding language as profoundly indeterminate; at bottom, history can no more be fixed than a poem. In this sense, by placing history into a literary context—that is, into a systematic aesthetic understanding of texts—New Criticism offers an alternative to the fixed meanings of technocratic culture. Brooks is referring to history in the broadest possible sense, but his pedagogy also suggests that in order to teach literature, we must understand another history at the level of the student's learning. The indeterminate epistemology of language is presented to students living quite determinate lives. Brooks's focus on "the poem itself," I would argue, is a pedagogical strategy, not a metaphysical argument about the nature of literature or language.

Brooks also implies that the question facing literary critics is not about the nature of literature or language but about student and social needs for specific forms of cultural capital. Bourdieu and Guillory provide support for the idea that this cultural capital was—and is—an important, even vital, source of social and economic power. Again, it is the hierarchy of aesthetic over ethos that ought to be dismantled, not the pedagogy of the formalist aesthetic as such. Indeed, if we believe that knowledge is in fact often misrepresented as fixed scientific fact, Brooks's concerns seem reasonable, even necessary. Moreover, this analysis reinforces the idea that a purely vocational education cannot provide the cultural capital needed for a middle-class way of life. To paraphrase Bourdieu, the economic game, to some extent, demands the system of distinctions systematized in a formalist aesthetic; successful class mobility is as much a matter of linguistic and aesthetic sensibility as it is of technical knowledge. In minimizing the formalist aesthetic, in other words, a professional education minimizes the critical efficacy of a college education. Insofar as a formalist aesthetic is a product of socioeconomic class, and so is inculcated through familial exposure, this elision of aesthetics in effect privileges the already privileged.

Brooks recognized that the reception and adoption of formalist aesthetic notions are dependent as much on social background and environment as on pedagogy and are lifelong endeavors. A habitus is never discretely achieved but accumulates dynamically. The goal of close reading, as Brooks emphasized, was to teach students a social process in which their reading could develop ever-finer distinctions: "In one of his letters, [Robert Penn] Warren told me that criticism for him was a social act; what he said he liked best was to get together with someone in a room who was different from him and read a play, novel, poem or whatever, and talk about it, and argue over it, and fight over it, and see where they agree or disagree. That, for him, was criticism" (Spurlin, Fisher, and Brooks 371). The well-wrought text is, in short, only a single moment in the larger evolution of the well-wrought professional. Fluency in a formalist aesthetic, for Brooks, would provide a kind of counterweight to the nominal certainties of the popular ethos.

To lift (and extend) a phrase from Janice A. Radway, students raised in families that know what and how to read are more likely to acquire the full range of cultural capital rewarded by the economic games of professionals. Students who do not come from such families will have a more difficult time; my father's case suggests that some did not completely succeed. The relative differences in the successful inculcation of the formalist aesthetic can thus serve as markers within the middle class, depending, as well, on the content and length of the professional program. A lawyer and a business major are both educated, but a lawyer is said to be more educated. It is important to note that in Bourdieu's view, cultural capital never simply or easily translates into economic capital; a business major might nevertheless end up making more money than a lawyer. A law degree, too, as my father's experience also illustrates, is more expensive, in terms of both time and money invested, and so socially and economically more distinctive. Yet the role of aesthetics in U.S. culture has been muddled by the ongoing debate over the aims, goals, and achievements of the New Critics. More recently, however, reconceptualizations of the history of New Criticism have begun to challenge this obscuration.

Conservative critics of the New Criticism, Carton and Graff have written, often presented the history of literary studies in the United States as an ongoing descent into irrelevance. Carton and Graff describe this traditional view as "a narrative of creeping academic professionalization, in which critics lose touch with the audience for literature and finally with literature itself" (282). The New Criticism is said to be opposed to a currently fashionable, elitist discourse, increasingly concerned with arcane issues that are of little or no interest to the public. The often explicitly politicized contemporary criticism stands out against a New Critical discourse said to be free of unnecessary jargon and concerned solely with literature in and of itself. For these critics, New Criticism ought to be held up as a model of the work of the literary professor and of the lucid explication that ought to lie at the heart of the field. Setting aside politics and jargon, these critics argue, is precisely what critics ought to do again.

Carton and Graff acknowledge the dangers of a "self-enclosure of theoretical discourse," accessible only to experts. Yet they also argue that this view presents the New Criticism as "less troubled and contentious than it really was, as well as more comfortably accessible to the general reader": "These alarmist tales are too strongly colored by a need to make scapegoats of today's theorists and have become the latest in a long line of resentments against the academic appropriation of literature that had originated much earlier" (282, 283). In this conservative storyline, then, Brooks is presented as the exemplar of a now compromised literary criticism in which critics spoke clearly and simply, and literary theory was both easy to understand and intellectually consensual. In fact, as Carton and Graff demonstrate, New Criticism arose out of an ongoing and often contentious debate among a variety of competing literary theorists and methodologies. And the New Critical vocabulary, which now seems self-evident, Carton and Graff note, was itself once thought to be an overly difficult, jargon-laden discourse inaccessible to a general audience. Again, my study reinforces this notion that literary education was far from simple in light of either disciplinary or student reception or in its socioeconomic import.

Brooks's views on pedagogy were consistent enough that he allowed an essay published in 1940, "What Are English Teachers Teaching?," to be republished in an abbreviated form in 1970. In a letter to the editor included as an introduction, Brooks laments that he has no time to expand his ideas but insists that the basics of the situation of the literary teacher remain unchanged: "If I were writing about it today, I would want to take into account some of the new features of our cultural and literary situation, but they do not involve, as I see it, any profound change in the state of affairs. I am perfectly willing to stand by, in essentials, what I wrote so many years ago" ("English Teachers" 5). Even the social upheavals of the time, Brooks implies, have not changed the fundamental need for teaching a formalist aesthetic.

For Carton and Graff, the important contrast to be drawn is between what critics in the 1940s saw as an "armchair amateurism" and a more sophisticated systematic critical practice. In the first three decades of the twentieth century, literary study, once dominated by the salon and the general interest magazine, found a home in the university and the academic journal: "What initially struck its contemporaries about the university criticism . . . was not that it was determinedly aesthetic and formalist but . . . that for the first time professors were producing criticism not as men of letters but as professionals" (292). Since the late 1940s, however, the multidisciplinary origins of the New Criticism have been obscured by the success of "the school described and exemplified by Brooks—critics who elevated the text itself above its sources and effects" (292). The success of Brooks's New Criticism is best understood, then, in terms of the dictates of "the departmentalized university, in which literary study is required to claim its own subject matter in order to legitimate itself as an academic field" (296). The New Criticism dominated academic criticism so fully "that the implication was that the 'intrinsic' analysis performed by Brooks and his school just simply was literary criticism—no other kind of criticism could really claim to be literary" (294).

Carton and Graff believe the historical record contradicts this conservative view of a consensual and unproblematic New Criticism. In the 1940s, Carton and Graff write, critics like Stanley Edgar Hyman saw "even the most aesthetically oriented versions of the new criticism [as] a type of interdisciplinary criticism that derives its central terms from the field of *linguistics*" (293; emphasis in original). The institutional pressure for professional legitimization and against "genteel impressionism" ensured that the intrinsic form—again, exemplified by Brooks—came to dominate both the image of New Criticism (as criticism itself) and the pedagogical practices of university-level literary education (295).

Interestingly, Brooks, too, argued against the "genteel impressionism" then common to critical discourse. In "Forty Years of Understanding Poetry," Brooks describes a well-known essay by William K. Wimsatt and Monroe Beardsley: "'The Affective Fallacy' does not say—as some scholars seem to think—that the reader shouldn't be affected by a poem or that the poem is a coldly intellectual process, a puzzle to be worked out. What the essay does argue is this: that to judge a poem by exclaiming 'Great' or 'Lovely' or 'Wow' is a very vague and unsatisfactory kind of criticism" ("Forty Years" 9). Brooks, while arguing for a systematic and so presumably intellectually legitimate study of literature, warns that this "professionalization" must also resist reducing pedagogy, and so criticism, to the "cold puzzle" of academic discourse. For Brooks, however, what is unsatisfactory about the amateur's "Wow" is that it fails to address the needs of those other amateurs, the students who, like my father, come to the classroom without much exposure to a formalist aesthetic. Arguably, it is these same needs that I would argue literary studies must learn to address if it hopes to once again pursue a progressive agenda relevant to its students lives, professional and otherwise.

4

Ethos, Avocation, and the Liberal Arts

> There is an economy of cultural goods, but it has a specific logic. Sociology endeavors to establish the conditions in which the consumers of cultural goods, and their taste for them, are produced. . . . But one cannot fully understand the cultural practices unless "culture" in the restricted, normative sense of ordinary usage is brought back into "culture" in the anthropological sense, and the elaborated taste for the most refined objects is reconnected with the elementary taste for the flavors of food.
>
> —Pierre Bourdieu, *Distinction*

SPOTTED HORSES

IN JANUARY 1981, on my father's fifty-eighth birthday, I sent him a collection of fiction by William Faulkner, *Spotted Horses and Other Stories*. It was one of my favorite southern literary texts at the time, and since Dad was from Mississippi, I felt sure he would enjoy it as well. I was living in Austin, a junior at the University of Texas busy with my studies, and like many young men too rarely found time to visit my family. Dad and I never talked about the book, and on July 3 of that same year, he died of what the coroner later determined was "hypertensive and arteriosclerotic heart disease." After the long holiday weekend, we gave him a veteran's funeral at the National Cemetery in Houston. We buried him in a coffin the color of his favorite car, a medium blue 1964 Dodge Dart. In accordance with military tradition, my mother was presented with a carefully folded American flag in honor of his service to his country. Over the course of this study, I have often thought of that book that I gave my father and of the conversation it implied, a dialogue interrupted by his death.

However inchoate my desires may have been at the time, it seems to me now that my choice of a gift had two important motivations.

First, I was seeking a way to introduce my father into the literary world—the languages and codes—that I had discovered as an English major. More important, I felt that Faulkner's shorter narratives might provide a kind of neutral ground on which we could explore my father's childhood and, perhaps, his experiences in the war. Like many veterans of his time, my father only rarely discussed his past. In terms of my subsequent research and understanding, what I find most significant is that I did not choose, say, a popular history of Mississippi in the 1930s or any number of similar texts on World War II. A text whose genre and form did not highlight language in any particular way, what I would now call a text that adhered to a strict communicative or popular ethos, seemed an inadequate framework for what I wanted to accomplish. On the other hand, I also understood that a text too deeply committed to experimentation or self-consciously shaped through a formalist aesthetic was equally inappropriate. My father would not have had the background in language, and interpretation and translation would have been a difficult, if not fruitless, exercise.

Rightly or wrongly, I believed that *Absalom, Absalom!* or *As I Lay Dying* would have been to a large degree incomprehensible to my father, despite their familiar epoch and setting. These texts depended on a kind of linguistic capital that I knew he had never accumulated. Put simply, I believed that the unfamiliar narrative forms would have made for a difficult, unproductive exchange. What I sought was a text through which we might have a conversation about the world and, to a lesser extent, about the language used to describe the world. As Cleanth Brooks might say, the intricate dynamics of our relationship, and my father's life, seemed to demand an aesthetic of language that accentuated—and perhaps explained—difficulty and ambiguity. A formalist aesthetic, by calling attention to the language itself, more closely corresponded to my sense that the past was not solely a matter of discovering facts or objective knowledge but also an encounter with form and style and voice. I wanted more than data about my father's life; I wanted to hear him tell his story in his own language, to hear it *slant*.

In academic terms, what I wanted was a kind of epistemological bridge between our disparate experiences and expectations about language. In my mind, Faulkner's short stories seemed the perfect vehicle, a blend of traditional narrative techniques and not-too-unconventional linguistic and formal style. Anyone who has taught an introductory literary course will be familiar with this search for a text that is challenging but not alienating, one that introduces students to a discussion rooted in a reflective appreciation of language and form. Most teachers, too, would agree that we are successful in our search only to the extent that we can establish a dialogue with our students; we have to judge how far we can take them before they simply drop out in frustration or confusion. The discussion I wanted to initiate with my father remains in this sense a model for my understanding of pedagogy. I wanted to explain to him what I had learned about language so that I could more fully understand what he had learned in his life. I was trying to cross a divide created by socioeconomic class and education, by time, place, and age, and by our differing opportunities for the investment of time and energy in language. In a sense, I am the interest my father received for his original college venture, and I wanted to return the favor.

I have always thought that teachers as much as writers have to see and know something of the world outside of the United States in order to be effective. If a person lived only in a relatively affluent corner of the American South, what did he or she really know? Of course, I didn't have much money of my own, so I had to work my way out of Texas. In 1986, soon after receiving an MA at UT Austin, I joined the Peace Corps, and after several weeks of training (ten days in San Francisco and then more than two months on the island of Samar), I lived and worked for two years in the small town of Conception, Philippines. The Aquino government, recently elected after the peaceful People's Revolution that deposed Ferdinand Marcos, would not allow Americans to teach Filipino students directly, so I spent my time in a variety of teacher training and public health programs.

After my service, I had no desire to go back to the United States and live under the Reagan regime, and so in late 1988 I traded in my return ticket and flew in the other direction, spending ten days each in Hong Kong, Bangkok, Thailand, and New Delhi. I came to ground in Paris just before Christmas, where I had arranged to meet a friend—an ex-girlfriend—who had spent the summer picking grapes in the south of France. Earlier in the year, I had met a man in the Vietnamese refugee camp on Luzon, improbably named Eugene Debbs, who told me that if I wanted to teach English in Paris, I should look up Jack McDougal, an Irish American expatriate who ran a small school catering to businesspeople. It was quite a change, working in Paris, and it took several meetings and a new suit to convince Jack that I would be a good employee, but I finally succeeded. Jack had hired returned Peace Corps volunteers before, so I had some social capital I could invest.

I worked at McDougal's English Language Study Group for nearly three years, holding small classes in French banks and accounting firms and teaching lessons on the telephone on long, intensive weekends. In 1991, I decided I was ready to return to the United States and complete my PhD. Since I had left, of course, changes in English studies had dramatically transformed what it meant to be a college professor. At the University of Texas, in particular, there had been the debacle of the Writing and Difference program in the late 1980s and the subsequent creation of the Department of Rhetoric and Composition out of the English department a few years later. The DRC created both the Writing Center and the Computer Writing and Research Laboratory. English studies as a whole had witnessed a similar shift in energy and resources away from literary studies and toward writing pedagogy, helped along by the birth of the World Wide Web and e-mail. Although my master's thesis had been on Paul de Man, I quickly realized that the real excitement and energy seemed to be emerging out of the relatively new field of rhetoric and composition. I settled into the routines of graduate school for much of the 1990s.

LEGITIMACY IN ENGLISH STUDIES

The field of rhetoric and composition, while in many senses strengthened by its increasing professionalization, faces a legitimacy crisis as a form of professional employment. Arguably, writing instruction is evolving toward a system in which a few more-or-less well-paid professors supervise a vast army of graduate students and adjuncts. Under such circumstances, full integration into classroom practices of the complex heritage of research already represented by rhetoric and composition is unlikely. The so-called economies of scale and exploitative labor practices attendant to large-scale education can only encourage a reductive pedagogical methodology. In this sense, to the extent that the liberal arts paradigm has begun to collapse into a narrowly defined vocational model, the standardized test is analogous to a narrowly defined current-traditional rhetoric focused on grammatical fidelity. The test as well as the rhetoric represent a denuded form of cultural capital drained of its existential, transformative potentials. The roots of these crises are foundational to the discipline of English studies in the United States, a field inexorably tied to its birth in depression and war and its maturation in the Cold War. English studies' dual rejection of both quotidian reality and collective bargaining has left it ill prepared for contemporary social realities.

Some maintain that technological change, in any case, has rendered much of the traditional methods of education in language and literature obsolete. Computers and e-mail, however, are in themselves largely means rather than ends, and contending that they are the key to the future of our discipline begs the question, "What makes up the cultural capital of English studies?" We will certainly be using these technologies; less certain is to what end or under what professional arrangements. What's more, the traditional forms of cultural capital in English studies, with its hierarchical professional and educational system that privileges the formal aesthetic over the popular ethos, are unlikely to return with anything like the force they once marshaled. The specific sociological conditions, in other words, in which the modern middle class was born no longer hold sway over the political and social conditions that shape higher education in the United States. If class mobility was the founding principle guiding access to universities in the twentieth century, class maintenance is increasingly becoming the norm today.

In recent years, reformers have attempted to reformulate the cultural capital of English studies in hopes of addressing these demographic changes and countering the alienation of a mass education system. In order to illustrate these phenomena, I begin the chapter with a discussion of Neal Lerner's analysis of the relationship between growth in enrollment and the use of student conferences. Lerner narrates a kind of fable of the push of humanization against the pull of the market. Lerner shows how, after the population boom of the late 1960s, teachers used conferences as an egalitarian measure, hoping to counter the traditionally teacher-centered classroom as well as the perceived alienation of mass education. This strategy, of course, was necessarily limited by the availability of capital, as Lerner emphasizes. In each case, teachers quickly understood that there were too few educators and too many students for this strategy to succeed. Similarly, Christopher Schroeder argues that the recent growth in enrollment has fed a continued sense of crisis and malaise in U.S. education that can only reinforce the perception that traditional academic forms are no longer legitimate. This sense of calamity, Schroeder contends, exacerbated by rapid technological and demographic change, is contemporaneous with the decline of literary studies as a dominant paradigm in English studies.

Literacy as modeled in the English department, Schroeder argues, is profoundly divorced from the realities of contemporary American society. More and more, he suggests, a student body both less white and more technologically savvy will be reluctant to accept what academics in English have to offer. Perhaps ironically, however, Schroeder believes that new communication technologies such as the World Wide Web and e-mail offer a way to reinvent English studies as a less estranged, more flexible discipline, better able to adapt to these changing conditions. Schroeder's technological solutions, however, don't fully address the question of what should or might be taught via these new media. Is traditional academic writing to be abandoned whole cloth in favor of blogs and e-mail? In hopes of finding an answer, I next turn to Bruce Horner's critique of the continuing trend away from long-established academic forms of writing. Horner's analysis of what he calls the "functionalist error," I contend, offers a useful counterweight to Schroeder's emphasis on technological and pedagogical reform, reminding us that alienation is rooted in the use of particular genres and methods rather than inherent to the genres and methods.

Horner's criticisms, I believe, are also particularly helpful in considering conventional views of vocational education, long denigrated as anathema to the liberal arts. I conclude this section with Russell Durst's extended discussion of writing pedagogy in *Collision Course*. Durst argues that academics have conventionally mistrusted the idea of an education oriented toward the kinds of instrumental language that most contemporary U.S. students seem to believe they need. Rather than resist or ignore these demands, Durst says, compositionists need to articulate what he terms a "reflective instrumentalism" that in effect meets students' class aspirations halfway. Clearly, students' demand for practicality in education and for the cultural capital represented by instrumental language and the popular ethos is overdetermined by the precarious position of the U.S. middle class in the current economy. Just as clearly, it would be irresponsible, I think, to ignore what Barbara Ehrenreich has called this "fear of falling."

Finally, a reformed English studies, if it is to avoid what Schroeder terms "socialization into a monolithic, universalized cultural capital" (6) and the fetishism identified by Horner, must have an ethnographic component. In the concluding section of this chapter, then, I attempt to articulate this new model for English studies, what I call a "writing in the wild" format, which emphasizes the contingency of writing and its dependence on the particularities of institutions, audiences, and purposes and which conceptualizes learning as a shared enterprise among teachers, students, and institutions.

TECHNOLOGY, GROWTH, AND THE CULTURAL CAPITAL OF ENGLISH STUDIES

Using data from the U.S. Department of Education, Neal Lerner has identified four dramatic periods of expansion in American higher education: 1879–80, when enrollment doubled; 1929–30, when enrollment increased by 84 percent; 1949–50, when it increased by 78 percent; and 1969–70, when it rose an astounding 120 percent. Among other things, Lerner contends, periods of rapid growth tend to generate a "desire for intimacy" that encourages the use of conferences as a way to counter the potential estrangement of mass education. The intimacy of individualized instruction offers a counterweight to the perceived impersonality of the large lecture hall. In this sense, the democratic impulse toward a humanistic, individualized education that could maximize the potential for the inculcation of cultural capital finds a moral and ethical voice inside a system whose logic is rooted in (amoral) economies of scale. Soon enough, however, teachers realize that there are limits to the numbers of conferences they can hold in any one semester. In every case, the turn toward individual instruction, Lerner notes, "was countered by the working conditions for faculty: too many students and too little time" (187). Here, as elsewhere, the capitalist economic system in the United States—with its periodic but limited willingness to invest in social mobility—operates in dynamic pressure with a democratic impulse toward increased access.

On the one hand, a variety of social forces—immigration, mass mobilization, economic depression, and war—can serve to push the system in a democratic direction, toward a wider, more inclusive distribution of cultural and economic capital. As more people have access to capital, the middle class expands. My father, of course, was fortunate enough to have been eligible for college during one of these periods of great expansion of opportunity. At the same time, a variety of countervailing social forces, founded in notions of the relative limits of capital and the long-term profitability of educational investment, limit the size and scope of the system through which capital is (re)distributed. As I have noted in my father's story, for example, the GI Bill excluded law school.

The United States has only rarely experimented with full access to education, of course, with its nominally high costs and potentially chaotic logistics, as it did for a brief time in a limited way after the 1969–70 expansion. Instead, traditional assessment methodologies provide a "natural" limit to the potentials for access to the cultural capital represented by a college education. These methodologies, of course, also provide a convenient, meritocratic smoke screen obscuring a more fundamental unwillingness to invest in a fully effective education system. Arguably, with enough time and individualized instruction, anyone could have a college degree. More profit lies elsewhere, however. Since educational capital derives its value to some degree from its relative scarceness, one might also suggest less charitable motives for so-called objective assessment.

More recently, Lerner writes, "the responses to the enrollment bulge of the late 1960s have given us a belief in conferences as a way of making the teacher-student relationship not necessarily more meaningful or more intimate but more equal" (202). The mass movements of the 1950s, 1960s, and 1970s—for civil rights, students, women, gays—also encouraged attempts to correct the perceived limitations of the system of higher education that these movements had helped to make more accessible. The limits of capital play a decisive role in a system rife with the potential for abuse and discontent. Economies of scale encourage large class sizes, for example, among other things; teachers may respond with conferences, but can go only so far, again, given the limits imposed by available capital. The availability of capital, of course, is in large part determined by the movements' political successes. Ironically, Lerner's analysis also suggests that teachers use conferences as a counterweight to their own institutional and professorial authority, often perceived as arbitrary if not capricious. Nevertheless, this notion of equality—that will eventually mature into so-called student-centered learning—became a defining ideological component of the system through which the cultural capital of English studies was distributed.

Christopher Schroeder, among others, has noted that the last decade of the twentieth century witnessed yet another growth spurt in student populations, a rise projected to continue for some time. Again, the rise in enrollment feeds a contemporary perception of crisis and undermines the traditional academic sense of legitimacy. Not surprisingly, this present-day expansion has also met nominal capital limits, accompanied by a dramatic increase in the use of standardized testing and adjunct labor. Schroeder also emphasizes that this new student population will be less white than their immediate predecessors and so face an additional potential for dissatisfaction. His argument begins with demographics of change:

> Of postsecondary institutions in the United States, the combined undergraduate population will increase by nineteen percent over the next decade or so from 13.4 million students in 1995 to 16 million students by 2015. More to my argument about legitimacy, of the additional 2.6 million students, more than two million will be minorities . . . thereby increasing the total number of minority students from 29.4 percent in 1995 to 37.2 percent in 2015. (3)

Schroeder further argues that rapid technological transformations exacerbate our sense of crisis. As a result of the development of computer-assisted communication in general and the Internet in particular, our contemporary quandary, Schroeder says, is uniquely less a matter of "skills and abilities and more a matter of meaning" that "reflect[s] . . . the illegitimacy of the cultural capital, or symbolic power, of intellectual work in the U.S. academy" (1). The rise of these technologies, in other words, has only deepened the rift between the work (of reading and writing) done outside of the academy and the educational priorities within. This rift, again, was founded on a traditional paradigm of English studies shaped by a strict disciplinary hierarchy in which the formal aesthetic, defined as the non-useful, was prioritized over the popular ethos.

What's more, Schroeder says, "the primary site of acculturation into these decontextualized literacies has been the English department" (1). Whatever else has changed, English studies, then, continues to play its historically central role in the U.S. university system, even if, in Schroeder's terms, that duty has largely gone awry. "Over time," Schroeder writes, "literacy instruction generally, and in the United States specifically, has authorized versions of literacy increasingly separated from the social and cultural contexts that make these literacies meaningful" (1). Citing John Schilb, among others, Schroeder contends that the rise of these decontextualized literacies parallels the decline of literature as a dominant paradigm in English studies and the rise of composition, which has now "assimilated the entire responsibility of certifying students in the literacies and cultures of the academy" (2). Drawing from both anecdote and an admittedly small sample of textbooks, Schroeder describes what he calls the "essayist literacies" of the academy in general and of composition/English studies specifically. These ways of reading and writing, Schroeder states, emphasize "truth values as opposed to rhetorical conditions" and posit a "positivistic and foundational world" that students are encouraged to see as "entirely expressible in texts" (2).

Some compositionists, of course, might be surprised to hear their discipline, with its well-established tradition of discussing the postmodern, described as emphasizing "truth values" over "rhetorical conditions." Yet I would argue that this pressure toward a "positivistic and foundational world" is profoundly overdetermined in a capitalist economy. In the terms I have used throughout this book, Schroeder's analysis simply reiterates the continuing (if not expanding) dominance of the popular ethos in English studies, an epistemology of language rooted in what James Berlin calls an objectivist rhetoric. It may also be true, of course, that the rhetoric of the discipline of rhetoric and composition, rooted in the academic systems that govern tenure, may have a quite different agenda from that of the textbooks Schroeder examines. Traditionally, of course, English studies have sought, in effect, to transform the language of non-white, non-middle-class students, instilling in them the habitus of the white middle-class professional. A contemporary student body, increasingly non-white and politically aware, Schroeder suggests, will be less inclined to accept this arrangement. Schroeder believes that "if we are to do more than declare another literacy crisis in the face of these changes in student population and communicative technologies, then we must provide alternatives to the violence of appropriating or being appropriated by the dominant literacies of the academy" (4).

Clearly, U.S. higher education in general and English studies in particular face a dramatic set of opportunities and challenges in the coming decades. Increasing—and increasingly heterogeneous—student populations coupled with nominally limited financial capital suggest the potential for a progressively impersonal and alienating system more and more distant from the quotidian world in which students live and work during and after their college experiences. In English studies, of course, the threat is felt most dramatically in the now maturing field of rhetoric and composition. The social contexts of knowledge use and production, in short, are far removed from the "hyper-rationality" of the standardized test. The same could be said, of course, of many composition textbooks. Lerner reminds us that while conferences reflect "our need to forge connections with our students, the kind of promise for teaching and learning that drew us to the profession in the first place" (205), there are limits to the ways that individual teachers can humanize mass education through this sort of individualization. In addition, as Schroeder also notes, citing Cynthia L. Selfe and Richard J. Selfe Jr., "the discursive powers of computers inscribe their own cultural biases by privileging capitalism, social class, standard English, rationalism and logocentrism" (6). Indeed, collective action, both inside and outside of the university, seems the only certain way to ensure the capital necessary to preserve and extend humanized education.

As the larger student population pushes for increased access, however, capital itself will surely pull back, arguing that the funding available for education is by definition limited. If we are to prevent the creation of a widely available but denatured form of cultural capital, then, we need to attempt to be as organized as capital itself. I return to this subject in some detail in my final chapter. Just as clearly, however, Schroeder is correct in arguing that new communicative technologies are helping to undermine the effectiveness of traditional, essayistic English-language pedagogy, if for no other reason than that they are creating new forms of literacy whose final shape or value has yet to be determined. Indeed, as the rise of social networking illustrates, any revision of English studies has to be both dynamic and profoundly adaptive. Whatever else a wiki may be, it is not a book; a blog may be essayistic, but it is not an essay; and while e-mail may belong to an epistolary genre, it is not a letter. Moreover, as computers and broadband become as ubiquitous—at least in the West—as telephones and televisions, the dynamics of access are shifting yet again. In the face of such change, Schroeder's call for an education into a less "monolithic, universalized cultural capital" in favor of a pedagogy that emphasizes "experiencing differences and experimenting with discourses, meanings and words" (6) seems both practical and necessary.

Our desire for humanistic education, however, must also contend with the long-standing historical conflict in U.S. education between vocational educational desires and purposes and the transformative potentials emphasized in the liberal arts. English studies, of course, embodies these tensions in the multiple professional and pedagogical differences that have shaped the histories of literary studies and rhetoric and composition. Insofar as vocationally oriented education is associated with "skills and abilities," many academics associate it with the worst aspects of large-scale education. I doubt that anyone would advocate a return to a more teacher-centered form of distribution. In addition, when business leaders and conservative politicians call for a more relevant education, they are in most cases relying on a rhetoric of vocational and professional employment. In contrast, the liberal arts have offered the promise of individualized instruction and transformation, perhaps epitomized within traditional English studies in the small-scale literary seminar.

In recent years, this conflict has often emerged as a tension between students' desires for an education pertinent to their immediate professional aspirations and their teachers' broader social goals. Students come to college, the cliché goes, to get a well-paying, secure job; professors teach, in contrast, in order to create critical thinkers and effective democratic citizens. In the field of rhetoric and composition, this tension has more recently fueled a response that Bruce Horner has described as rooted in a powerful "ambivalence" toward traditional academic pedagogy.

> Academic discourse . . . is rejected as too constraining, as ill equipped to represent the range of thoughts and experiences that students and their teachers bring to the composition course; the concerns traditionally expressed in academic discourse pale in comparison to concerns of real political, economic, and/or personal significance for teachers, students, and the public at large. (169)

This work, Horner suggests, represents an attempt to reinvent the academic in order to address the perceived disconnection between the classroom and the world and so address the ongoing potential for irrelevance if not alienation. "Against academic work," Horner writes, "these writers pose work that is seen as social, real, experience-based, committed" (169). The service-learning course, then, like the conference, represents an attempt to counter the potential dehumanization of education by breaching the protective walls of the school.

THE MESSY BUSINESS OF CLASS MOBILITY

The problem with such approaches, Horner notes, is that they tend to reinforce what he calls a "functionalist error," which "confuses the denigration . . . of skills and those using them with the skills themselves" (173), in effect equating menial tasks with menial people. For Horner, these attempts to recontextualize education too often toss the baby out with the bathwater. "It is . . . not academic forms in themselves," Horner writes, "which have properties of impersonality and removal from social concerns. To believe so is to engage in commodity fetishism. Rather it is the dominant's reification of academic, and other, discursive forms that is to be combated: the treatment of these as fixed in meaning, purpose, and use, unsusceptible to human labor" (182). According to Horner, academics who are ambivalent toward what Schroeder calls "essayistic literacies" should seek ways to move "the focus of the composition course from discursive forms in themselves to the responsibilities and practices of readers and writers, and to the conditions making possible those practices and the work to which readers and writers so situated may put them" (183). In Horner's view, academic forms—"the seemingly impersonal academic report or essay" (181)—are not in themselves alienating or impersonal but simply tools that can be put to a variety of uses in a variety of contexts. The same computer used in the exploitative workplace could be used to communicate more effectively a local community group's fight for justice. Essays or reports, too, have been used to pursue nondominant agendas. Similarly, as Horner notes, service-learning courses can simply become another item on a résumé. The question, then, is not so much about which tools or kinds of texts are the most alienating as it is about how these tools and discourses are used, by whom, and to what end.

In our current environment, I would argue that Horner's analysis also suggests a corollary principle: we must avoid fetishes for traditional academic forms as well as for their historical opposites, essays as much as memos. It is on the terrain of the useful and the practical, I would argue, and of professional relevance, that contemporary education will either rise or fall. Vocational education, in other words, long held suspect in the traditions of the liberal arts, can also be understood in terms of "the responsibilities and practices of readers and writers" rather than as a denatured set of "skills and abilities." In this light, as I hope I have made clear, the popular ethos appears as intellectually challenging and sophisticated as the formalist aesthetic.

In this sense, the traditional hierarchy of literary studies over composition rests on a kind of fallacy in which art trumps communication. Horner's analysis, then, also suggests an important, if perhaps implicit, question relevant to any class-based understanding of education. In our attempts to maintain humanistic education and to create relevant, humanistic pedagogies that incorporate changing technologies and epistemologies, do we need to ignore our students' more pragmatic desires and goals? If we pursue a pedagogy that emphasizes Schroeder's new literacies, are we simply furthering the long-standing conflict between the liberal and the useful arts, attempting to shift the historical priority of the former to the latter? Does an emphasis on new communications technologies necessarily also suggest either a wholesale rejection of academic tradition or a capitulation to a narrow vocational orientation?

Russell Durst's recent book-length study, *Collision Course*, explores these questions in some detail, implicitly arguing against what I would call a kind of sentimental egalitarianism that would collapse the important differences between the often-conflicting agendas of teachers and students. Teachers, after all, are influential by virtue of their (relatively rare) possession of the very sorts of knowledge and cultural capital students are ostensibly seeking through an education.

What separates teacher from student is as much a matter of an irreducible investment of time and energy—embodied capital, among other things—as it is of goals and purposes. Rather than pursue what could be only an illusory equality, Durst implies, we should develop strategies of just negotiation and persuasion. What's more, the most significant inequity concerns teachers' and students' differing commitments to the traditions of liberal education. In recent years, Durst writes, American students have seemed to "focus more and more on issues of financial security and worries about economic uncertainty" (170). Too often, composition specialists "have been slow to recognize the pervasive pragmatism of college students and of U.S. society more generally" (170).

Rather than simply reassert the importance of the liberal arts paradigm and fight against student pragmatism, Durst contends that compositionists should attempt to articulate a pedagogical philosophy rooted in what he calls "reflective instrumentalism." While recognizing the "major down side" of instrumental notions of composition, Durst says, we also have to accept that it is "too deeply ingrained in U.S. culture and history to be . . . blithely ignored" (174). Indeed, these aspirations are rooted in a desire for class mobility that has long shaped U.S. education. In addition, as teachers, we are ourselves profoundly and inescapably dependent on instrumental language:

> As a society we all benefit from the work of engineers, architects, computer hardware and software designers, accountants, business managers, scientists, pharmacists, teachers, health care professionals, and artists of various kinds. Every time I log onto my computer, search the Internet, ride my bicycle, watch a film, listen to my compact disk player, cross a bridge, ride an elevator, or relax in my own home, I am enjoying the fruits of instrumentalism. (175)

In the classroom in particular, Durst says, the academic anti-instrumentalist bias too often results in "more than a hint of intellectual elitism—a belief in the superiority of the critical, intellectual work of academics over other kinds of work" (175). As a result, we are less effective at instilling in our students the desire for knowledge as such that is the ostensible goal of the liberal arts as traditionally conceived.

The very structure of English studies, this analysis suggests, with its hierarchical denigration of a popular ethos, effectively undermines the less immediately practical educational goals we want our students to pursue. In denigrating the popular ethos and instrumental language, we also obscure the messy business of class mobility, with its unstable mix of existential and material desire and individual and social aspirations. Ironically, in portraying the transformative agenda of the liberal arts as diametrically opposed to vocation, we encourage the very alienation we wish to counter. Even more, the academic bias against instrumentalism reflects a deeper suspicion of avocation. Given the increasing power of capital over labor in recent years and the progressively more precarious status of the middle class in the United States, it seems unsurprising that students' agendas place a particular emphasis on a pragmatic concern with their financial well-being.[1] Nonetheless, the dynamic identified by Durst is not a uniquely contemporary phenomenon, however tight the noose in recent times, but a tension with deep historical roots in the relationships among education, democracy, and class mobility in the United States.

English studies has historically sought to propagate a middle-class habitus rooted in a complex, even contradictory way of understanding language and the production of knowledge. Among other things, this habitus assumed the differing profitableness of the characteristic forms of cultural capital promulgated in the English department classroom. Literary studies, of course, has a less immediately practical application; composition was a site of pragmatic acquisition. Taken in its entirety, then, English studies embodies the notion that a habitus, like class mobility in general, is a process of accretion, a dynamic, even contradictory set of linguistic tastes accumulated over the course of a lifetime rather than achieved once and for all in the college classroom. Professionally, however, English studies has historically privileged literary knowledge, elevating the nominally impractical, analytic knowledge promulgated through the pedagogy of close reading. Among other things, this ideology of literary status denigrates the immediate, material, communicative purpose associated with a popular ethos—what Durst calls instrumental language.

Arguably, the lesser status of the popular ethos in particular and of writing instructors generally continues to play a significant role in the creation and maintenance of the academic distrust of instrumentalism and the communicative or popular ethos. But, as I have argued at some length, this tension between vocation and instrumental language and the nominally existential aims of literary studies and the liberal arts is in no sense an incidental phenomenon. On the one hand, a college degree would get one a better paying, less physically dependent job and so a better life; on the other, it would transform one into a critical thinker, a refined, articulate, and independent citizen. Once educated, too, a person would continue to educate himself or herself. This was always the promise of the university in general and of English studies in particular. The goals of a liberal education, however, can seem to contradict the practical desires associated with the material dimensions of class mobility, particularly in times of economic and social stress. In this sense, my father's time parallels our own. Research into contemporary student attitudes about education, Durst says, shows that they "tend to interpret the critical literacy approach as pessimistic, negative, and accusatory . . . at a time when they are trying hard to sustain the optimism and motivation necessary to do the hard work being asked of them" (176). The needs of a democratic society can contradict the economic goals of the individual; the existential agendas of the liberal arts may appear to be at odds with the professional and economic aspirations of the middle and working classes.

Seen in the larger context of contemporary U.S. society and of the relationship between class and education, these tensions hardly seem surprising. Given the importance of the accumulation of linguistic capital to students' future security and well-being, it's reasonable that they would resent any obstacles that seem unnecessary. Under pressure, the seemingly long-term returns of the liberal arts agenda may well be the first to be set aside. Alternatively, as in the case of my father, these goals may be seen as more appropriate to a future, more financially stable generation. Indeed, a teacherly insistence on so-called critical thinking might even seem naive to a student whose main motivation for being in college is to avoid ending up working for minimum wage in a repetitive, meaningless job. We cannot deny the power of these motivations, even when they are the poorly articulated and barely conscious fears of young adults. The origins of such anxieties have deep roots in the historical experiences of the working classes in the United States. Perhaps most important, then, in sharply distinguishing the liberal arts from the vocational, the critical from the professional, is that we risk denaturing both, suggesting that we cannot be practical in our pursuit of knowledge and that critical thinking has no place in everyday life.

How can we bridge this divide between personal and social transformation and individual well-being? Must the goals of the liberal arts remain in conflict with the vocational purposes and desires, the material and social class aspirations, embodied in the ideals of a university education? Durst argues that a pragmatic approach to educating students need not be uncritical or unselfconscious about the ills of our larger society. What compositionists need, Durst concludes, is a pedagogy that "preserves the intellectual rigor and social analysis . . . without rejecting the pragmatism of most first year college students" (178). Although Durst's candor is admirable and his open embrace of the popular ethos refreshing, I think it is important to acknowledge the risk of simplification implicit in his argument. Even America's notorious pragmatism has to be inflected differently in different times and places; the vocational desires of a community college student in the Midwest should not be equated with those of an English major at Berkeley, even as a freshman. Nevertheless, the dynamics of class and class mobility—the fear of falling—surely provide some of the energy behind this species of student resistance to difficult intellectual work in almost any institutional context.

Arguably, then, while Durst's work represents an implicit recognition of the realities of class as they are played out in the composition classroom, his analysis stops short of a full recognition of the myriad ways that the hierarchical structure of U.S. education affects students. Indeed, as class divisions in U.S. society and education intensify, these differences may become even more striking. Already the social and curricular gap between the Ivy League and the community college seems unbridgeable. Nevertheless, Durst's framework of analysis serves as a useful and too rare reminder that instrumentalism cannot be summarily dismissed as "philistine" or as merely the reflection of commercial interests. To invoke Horner, we cannot fetishize the popular ethos any more than the formalist aesthetic. Indeed, the fetishistic elevation of the formalistic aesthetic created the nominal irrelevance of English studies. Instrumental language, too, is a matter of practices and people; it does important work in the world for labor and democracy as well as for capital and property. Students' ambitions for financial stability (if not prosperity) are as legitimate as our own desire to promote lifelong learning. Indeed, as professionals, those same academics who decry instrumental language have in part achieved their own status through a mastery of a communicative or popular ethos. Having already earned the capital of a popular ethos, in other words, academics can too easily forget the struggles that accompany its accumulation, particularly for those not born into relatively affluent, educated families. Durst's notion of a compromise between student and teacher emphasizes that our pedagogy ought to respect the legitimacy of our students' economic and social desires. Again, as professionals we may well share these goals.

ACADEMIA, THE POPULAR ETHOS, AND THE WRITING PROCESS

The key division or tension between composition and literary pedagogy and the hierarchical structuring of their differing epistemologies and ways of understanding language have shaped English studies throughout its modern history. As Durst suggests, this has led to the (academic, institutional) denigration of instrumental writing, what I have called the popular ethos, as intellectually insubstantial. This depreciation has, in turn, led to a history of professional exploitation. The perceived linguistic challenges of the formalist aesthetic—with its need for a relatively high investment of time and energy in its decoding and use—are directly related to higher salaries and the protections of tenure. Adjuncts and graduate students teach composition, thus freeing up economic capital to shore up the failing fortunes of literary studies. As Durst also implies, students are aware at some level that these linguistic and epistemological values are, in many ways, reversed outside of the classroom; thus their impatience with critical literacy. An investment in the popular ethos and instrumental language, in other words, is thought to return the highest yields in the employment market. Under current political and social conditions, the transformative traditions of the liberal arts may indeed appear irrelevant to students' social and economic aspirations; in contrast, it seems obvious that instrumental language can be invested at a relatively high rate of return.

Arguably, the more pressured a student's status, the greater his or her fear of falling, the more valuable a communicative ethos will seem, and the less pressing the desire for the existential transformations of literary studies in particular and the liberal arts in general. In this way, the dynamics of class mobility and struggle help to shape curricula, educational experience, and the accumulation of capital in different ways, depending, among other things, on the conditions associated with any particular sector of the institutional hierarchy. It seems reasonable to assume, to cite an obvious example, that once a student has won acceptance to an Ivy League school, questions of economic and social security recede, at least to some degree. Again, these assumptions about language, writing, and education have a wide circulation in U.S. society and have to be understood in terms of social and historical contexts well beyond the confines of the school. I would like to agree, then, with Durst that instrumentalism, or what I have called the popular ethos, is in fact both a legitimate focus for a critical pedagogy and an intellectually substantive endeavor. In this sense, we need not apologize for our desire to negotiate with students rather than to simply dismiss their desire for the capital represented by a popular ethos.

Even more important, Durst's analysis invites compositionists to put vocational and critical goals into a productive rather than an adversarial relationship. This, I would argue, has to be a key principle of the curricular reforms accompanying the institutional transformations that would support the full professional status of rhetoric and composition. Professional reform cannot succeed without accompanying intellectual and pedagogical change. A department composed of equal parts compositionists and literary specialists, in other words, should neither reproduce nor reverse an uncritical division between the vocational and the liberal arts, the popular ethos and the formalist aesthetic. In the context of contemporary U.S. culture and politics, composition's rise as an equal partner in English studies risks the institutionalization of a denatured capital rooted less in linguistic and so existential transformation and understanding than in the most narrowly defined vocational skills.

The risk of this hollowing-out increases exponentially as one moves down the educational hierarchy. A Harvard or Yale will always have the capital necessary to provide the transformative experiences of a liberal education; community and junior colleges may be not as fortunate. Across the broad base of the socioeconomic pyramid, students struggle to acquire the linguistic cultural capital they need to better themselves economically or to enter the professional classes. At the sharp tip, a relatively privileged few, having long ago acquired this capital at home and in financially flush public and private schools, debate postmodern literary forms and the historical rhetoric of postcolonial liberation movements. If English studies attempts to ameliorate the hierarchy of aesthetics and ethos, then, it will also have to address both existential and pragmatic educational purposes at every level. One size increasingly will not fit all.

Yet it is also important to emphasize that instrumental language is always more than a matter of simple grammatical fidelity. We need a reflective ethos of language embracing the complexities of communicative or instrumental writing as a worthy object of contemplation, an end as well as a means. We have to begin to search out ways to persuade our students that language and writing, aesthetic, communicative, instrumental, or otherwise, is always worth thinking about with craft and care. Here we can begin to confront the alienation that lies at the heart of mass education, the abstracted, rationalized models of knowledge that seem so distant from the material and social aspirations of our students. This is not to denigrate the importance of smaller classes, student-centered pedagogy, and conferences. It is to say, however, that before we can talk about how we can structure "critical reflection" into our writing instruction, we have to define in specific terms what we mean by the pedagogy of instrumental writing. How do we attempt to inculcate the popular ethos in the contemporary classroom? What do we teach when we teach a communicative or popular ethos in the English department? What would a writing pedagogy look like that resisted the dehumanization of commodified education and academic forms while remaining flexible enough to accommodate changing technologies and demographics? In particular, I believe that the writing process, with its open-ended, recursive, social process of discovery and invention, can stand as our humanistic, transformative alternative to the mechanized learning of the standardized test.

I would argue that in the last twenty years, research into writing pedagogy has begun to settle into a practical, concise classroom mode—a praxis of the writing process—that I would characterize in the following ways. First, our representation of the writing process has three main elements: effective writers go through drafts; they work collaboratively as much as they do individually; and they are reflective in their practices. As a result, writing teachers commonly ask students to go through a multidraft process, to do peer critiques, and to write self-assessments of various kinds. Importantly, our awareness that language and writing are context-bound in foundational ways can usefully complicate these truisms, helping to prevent them from becoming rigid formulas. Summarizing recent writing-across-the-curriculum thinking, for example, Thomas L. Hilgers, Edna Lardizabal Hussey, and Monica Stitt-Bergh write that "practitioners shifted attention from general goals and general processes to the particulars that define situations as unique, underscoring the post-modern view that every setting is best seen in terms of its 'situatedness'" (318). This suggests that context shapes both processes and product in profound ways. A peer critique between students in the classroom is one thing, the relationship between a lawyer/writer and his or her administrative assistant/editor or proofreader quite another. This context-bound knowledge demands that students become problem-solvers able to "learn strategies they can successfully apply in future circumstances" (Hilgers, Hussey, and Stitt-Bergh 348).

"What might it take to help students achieve proficiency," Hilgers, Hussey, and Stitt-Bergh ask, "as writers, thinkers and problem solvers?" (348). Teachers, the authors write, must have several interrelated goals:

> First, they must help each student situate each new research and writing task among prior experiences and thus to "discover" familiar strategies they might employ to accomplish the new task. Second, the instructors must foreground the processes of inquiry and validation that professionals in the field use to accomplish the new task. Third, they must help students come to see connections among inquiry methods, the recording of findings, and the processes of composing a final report. (348)

The "situatedness" of writing extends well beyond process. The assessment of product is as contingent as the pedagogy of process. We teach students to be concise, for example, even though we are aware that this term means subtly different things to professors, students, public school teachers, journalists, and advertising executives. The communicative ethos that underlies our sense of instrumental language is, ideally, richly strategic rather than narrowly formulaic.

What's more, even our truisms regarding the writing process are embedded in social context and historical circumstance, particularly if we consider writing practices more broadly than the traditional academic context might suggest. Perhaps a nurse writes the drafts of a medical report, for example, while its titular author, the doctor or head nurse, supplements his text with varying degrees of consultation. Alternatively, it may be a graduate student research assistant completing a report from blank page to publication, with her collaborator, the nominal scientist, doing nothing more than attaching his name to the finished document. In the final analysis, we define what we mean by a writing class through our characterization of the writing process, and through this designation, we shape students' expectations: whatever else this class is about, it will include drafts, peer critiques, and self-reflective exercises. At the risk of restating a cliché, instrumentalism in contemporary writing pedagogy, in other words, is less a product than a process. The school, however, with its logistical and financial demands and its textbooks and test scores and economies of scale, tends to emphasize product. Our arguments about contingency, then, must confront the inertia of so-called objective assessments and schools profoundly distorted by the economies of scale.

In addition, unless students have some opportunity to test and refine these principles outside of their particular classroom context, our truisms risk stifling the kinds of creative plasticity and innovation we know is as important in successful writing of all kinds as it is in critical thinking. Indeed, given the importance of the workplace in everyday life, testing and balancing the practices and relationships of the school against those of the workplace and the world at large—and vice versa—is arguably one of the most important critical thinking exercises we can offer. I would contend, then, that a pedagogy that emphasizes a living, communicative ethos—a recursive, collaborative, and reflective process—must necessarily also include an ethnographic dimension, underlining the importance of what John Seely Brown has termed, recalling Horner's "practices of writers," the tacit aspect of learning. "The explicit dimension," Brown has written, "deals with concepts—the 'know-whats'—whereas the tacit deals with 'know-how,' which is best manifested in work practices and skills. Since the tacit lives in action, it comes alive in and through doing things, in participation with each other in the world." Instrumentalism, in short, if it is to avoid Schroeder's "socialization into a monolithic, universalized cultural capital," as well as the fetishism of writing genre, has to maintain a productive engagement with writing outside of the classroom setting.

For example, instead of teaching a definition of concision, which will not always hold in the variety of situations and subjects in which students write, we need to find ways to teach concision (or clarity) in situ, ways of deciphering the meaning and efficacy of key concepts as they relate to specific situations, purposes, and audiences. Again, the focus should be on "practices and responsibilities" rather than on discursive forms as such. How does a police officer, for example, decide what will be most clear to the prosecuting attorney in his report? Similarly, students must learn a writing process strategy, a way to approach any potential writing task in terms of the design of the steps of its production. How do teachers, parents, social workers, and students collaborate in the production of individual education plans in the special education classroom? In meeting our students halfway, then, as Durst suggests should be our goal, we ought to be sending them out into the world in search of that irreducible complexity that our institutions too easily disallow. We have to find ways to persuade them that the capital they seek, indeed that we wish them to have, turns out to be more complicated than advertised.

I would like to argue, then, that the debate over the current crisis has begun to suggest an increasingly clear direction for reform in English studies, a set of goals rooted in this emerging paradigm of a complex, situated writing process. This reformist agenda has been shaped by the long-standing, humanistic insistence on the importance of small-scale, individualized education and on broadening access to the cultural capital of higher education. It should go almost without saying that among the most important elements of the emerging forms of cultural capital is a facility with new communication technologies. The new modus operandi of English studies, too, ought to be ethnographic in perspective, resisting the fetishism of both academic and non-academic forms of discourse, focusing on the practices of writers, and exploiting the tensions between work and school. The new models, I would argue, ought to turn their attention away from the classroom (without abandoning it or its forms of discourse) and move toward the workplace (without simply reproducing its practices as self-evident). This new paradigm would seek to reinvent and reenergize the relationship between work and school, the quotidian and the ideal, the academic and the vocational. Somewhat ironically, in my classes I have come to call my understanding and implementation of this new paradigm the "writing in the wild" model.

"Writing in the wild" is an allusion to the thesis of Edwin Hutchins's 1995 book, *Cognition in the Wild*. Hutchins is a cognitive anthropologist interested in exploring mental processes in real-life settings, here, in the context of the navigation of ships. Briefly, Hutchins contends that cognition in the wild is simply too complex a phenomenon to be reduced to the knowledge said to be "contained" in the minds of the sailors. Instead, he shows, cognition is best described as distributed across the environment in which it occurs. The thought or knowledge necessary to guide the ship into port, Hutchins says, is contained as much in the layout of the control room and in the maps as it is in the navigators' minds. Hutchins's work is richly suggestive of a variety of issues paramount to writing instruction. Perhaps most important, the distributive model provides a way to understand classroom, teacher, and student in terms of a complex, interdependent web of thinking and writing and technology, old and new. The "writing in the wild" model serves as a reminder to students that writing, like all knowledge, is situated, embedded in a particular context, rather than absolute.

WRITING IN THE WILD

In concluding this chapter, then, I would like to outline some of the ways that I have attempted to implement this new paradigm at several levels of instruction, from freshman to senior courses. What are the principles of this new, progressive paradigm? In a sense, the "writing in the wild" model can be thought of as a series of balancing acts. On the one hand, we must accept our students' vocational goals as legitimate expressions of their desire to maintain or strengthen their socioeconomic position; on the other, we must seek out ways to persuade them that the contemplative, reflective traditions of the academy are important to their professional and social futures. Indeed, our goals ought to be even larger: to convince students that despite their apparent impracticality, the critical methodologies of the school have immediate professional application. Alertness to injustice isn't simply helpful in "society in general"; it is necessary in the immediate, specific context of the work site.

Over the course of the last five years, I have gradually constructed a model that incorporates these principles in different ways, depending on the level of the course. The "writing in the wild" pedagogical framework emphasizes the contingency of knowledge about writing practices and de-centers learning by putting explicit knowledge into a productive tension with tacit learning. In effect, it serves to complicate what might well become the too simplistic representations we rely on as pedagogical and programmatic necessities. In summarizing his ideas about learning, Brown recalls Jerome Bruner: "The developmental psychologist Jerome Bruner made a brilliant observation years ago when he said we can teach people about a subject matter like physics—its concepts, conceptual frameworks, its facts—and provide them with explicit knowledge of the field, but *being* a physicist involves a lot more than getting all the answers right at the end of each chapter." I would argue that while we may not be able to eliminate the methods of the school or the academic forms of knowledge associated with it, we can complicate the classroom experiences of such "answers . . . at the end of each chapter" by seeking out ways of putting students into an effective rapport with tacit knowledge.

In this sense, Hutchins's ideas can also help to break down an overly atomistic way of conceptualizing learning and teaching. Quite literally, we are all in this together—thinking or knowledge in the classroom is framed as distributed across the learning environment, the technology, and the participants. The question, of course, is how to embody Hutchins's model in classroom practice. In my first-year writing course, this is accomplished through a linked series of assignments that guide students through an educational narrative that connects their own interests and desires to that of their families and then to the community at large. These assignments include several different genres of writing—a memoir in the form of an annotated bibliography, an interview with family members, and a demographic report, among others. Each assignment attempts to create opportunities for students to forge connections between their disparate experiences in and out of school. We begin, for example, with an annotated bibliography of texts that they feel have played an important role in their lives. Students learn to use classic academic skills such as summary and MLA formatting in order to provide a framework for understanding their own literate experiences.

In a more advanced "writing in the wild" classroom, students develop ideas about several different writing practices simultaneously through a semester-long research project on the work of a writer of their choice. Several may be studying the writing of teachers; others, firefighters or preachers. They begin their projects with a series of essays I have chosen in order to illustrate various ways of investigating writing. I have often used essays by bell hooks, for example, to initiate conversations about class, race, and gender. Other essays might focus on issues more specifically related to the writing process or to collaboration in a professional context. Students are encouraged to use these discussions as a base on which they can construct their own projects.

In this way, my courses implicitly argue that the practices of writing that students need to understand can be understood only in their "native" environment. Hutchins's work also suggests, of course, that students might best be served by being sent out into the world to study the ways that writers go about producing texts for particular audiences and purposes in specific situations and institutional settings. Just as Hutchins used a field research methodology to test the validity of cognitive theory, in other words, students use a similar field-based methodology to test our theories of writing and language and culture. The "writing in the wild" format, then, supports a richly recursive process in which students learn to write by writing about their investigations of writers. What's more, this model de-centers the classroom by asking students to bring to the classroom knowledge that they themselves have developed. Indeed, one of the most challenging—and exciting—aspects of this strategy is the way students continually teach me about writing as a contemporary social practice and phenomenon.

As a teacher, I offer students what are, after all, only theories, however well-tested; the "writing in the wild" model implicitly argues that these theories are not to be accepted passively but to be tested actively by the students themselves. At times, this testing occurs even with the most fundamental principles. Students, for example, who may believe that writing plays only a small role in their chosen field can examine their assumptions in a professional setting. With few exceptions, of course, they return to the class impressed at the key role writing will play in their working lives. The thinking done in this course is, in this sense, quite literally distributed among teachers, students, and the writers who are the research subjects. The thinking we do, in other words, lies at the intersection of the theories and experience I bring to the classroom and the differing ideas and data the students bring in from the world at large. In a concrete way, students and I make knowledge together through a complex negotiation between our competing interests. I might offer a definition of concision to my students, for example, but that definition is then tested—and modified, if not refined—by students through observation and interviews with writers. I might offer texts that make arguments about the collaborative process, which students can test in their own investigations. In writing about their research subject, too, they can then develop their own concision strategies appropriate to their developing understanding of texts, writers, and audiences. I could list dozens of examples of this sort, but suffice it to say that my students have found that writing clear, concise prose is fully dependent on context.

Students quickly adapt an idea that we teachers may only suspect is true: a lawyer is not concise in the same way as a professor or a public school teacher or a police officer. Indeed, a public school teacher may have several operative definitions of concision: one in play whenever she writes to her students, another when she writes to her principal, and yet another when she writes to the parents of her students. Each of these operant definitions, in turn, may be further refined by a teacher's desire to communicate or persuade or by her awareness of significant differences in the class, race, and gender of her students, parents, and colleagues. Similarly, lawyers or government officials may have radically different ideas of clarity and style, depending on their degree of commitment to what is called the plain language or plain English movement. When students are asked to investigate on their own and to share their findings through written and oral reports, contingency quickly becomes more than a teacher's theory.

The "writing in the wild" framework has three central elements, which I believe can reinvigorate English studies by reconnecting its practices to the world outside of the classroom. First is the representation of the writing process as knowledge-making—involving the production of drafts, some degree of collaboration among students, and periodic self-reflection exercises in which students articulate their sense of themselves as writers. Second is the de-centering influence of new communication technologies; ideally, students rely heavily on e-mail for the exchange of papers and information and, if possible, construct Web sites, loosely defined as online portfolios of their research projects. Third are the ethnographic elements, which allow students to explore the tacit dimensions of knowledge and which helps to emphasize the distributed nature of the knowledge we are making. In a single classroom, students may share information about writing from a range of quite different professions, exploring similarities and differences among writerly practices. The "writing in the wild" classroom is a nexus of information about writing brought in from the field, an overlapping set of concerns shared by teachers, copywriters, firefighters, and teachers, among many others. It is here among the mutual interests of classroom and profession that English studies can begin to regain its sense of legitimacy.

5

English Studies in an Age of Reform

> Of course, there is a portion of reading quite indispensable to a wise man. History and exact science he must learn by laborious reading. Colleges, in like manner, have their indispensable office,—to teach elements. But they can only highly serve us, when they aim not to drill, but to create; when they gather from far every ray of various genius to their hospitable halls, and, by the concentrated fires, set the hearts of their youth on flame. Thought and knowledge are natures in which apparatus and pretension avail nothing. Gowns, and pecuniary foundations, though of towns of gold, can never countervail the least sentence or syllable of wit. Forget this, and our American colleges will recede in their public importance, whilst they grow richer every year.
>
> —Ralph Waldo Emerson, *The American Scholar*

A GEOGRAPHY OF CRISIS

INCREASINGLY, LITERARY STUDIES HAS HAD particular difficulty defining its place in the landscape of educational aims and goals associated with class mobility and aspiration in contemporary U.S. society. If current developments continue unchallenged, the discipline of literary studies, as conventionally conceived, risks the historical fate of Latin or linguistics: pursued by advocates, and perhaps valuable in its own right, but largely irrelevant to the education of the majority of undergraduate and graduate students. As John Guillory and many others have argued, it no longer seems clear, as it did at midcentury, that a familiarity with literature is an important component of a middle-class sensibility in a democratic society. Many also argue that the habitus of the U.S. middle class has evolved beyond its mid-twentieth-century apprehensions about national culture.

Similarly, art in the traditional sense no longer seems the exemplary product of a triumphant American nation. Indeed, to many, the arts embody a suspect if not decadent liberalism; in any budget crunch in the public schools, they are the first to go. Among progressives, the very idea of transforming sensibility, or of taste, sounds imperial at best, racist or ethnocentric at worst.

As I argued in the previous chapter, English studies must be divorced from its twentieth-century habits of isolation and disengagement and reinvent itself as a subject with a productive, dynamic relationship with the culture it both investigates and serves. Literary studies, perhaps more so than any other activity in English studies, has a long way to go if it is to achieve a living reengagement with U.S. society. Curricular reform, moreover, cannot address the more fundamental institutional problems facing the contemporary U.S. university system, including the loss of autonomy in intellectual work and the professional devolution of the professoriat. Theoretically, any course, in other words, however progressive, can be taught by non-tenured adjuncts working full- or part-time. Legitimacy in English studies, then, is as much a matter of democratic self-organization in academia as it is relevant and engaging subject matter. English studies has lost both institutional power and prestige. How did the discipline lose the legitimacy that once underwrote its privileged status, at least for those at the top of the educational hierarchy? Can English studies regain the intellectual autonomy necessary for academic effectiveness?

I begin my exploration of these questions with a reading of four influential texts, each of which has contributed to the ongoing discussion of the future of English studies. These include Wlad Godzich's *Culture of Literacy*; James E. Seitz's *Motives for Metaphor: Literacy, Curriculum Reform, and the Teaching of English*; Richard E. Miller's *As If Learning Mattered: Reforming Higher Education*; and Stephen Parks's *Class Politics: The Movement for the Students' Right to Their Own Language*. Taken together, I would argue, these texts illustrate the rhetoric and ideologies of reform, a kind of geography of crisis, that have played such an important role in English studies as it moves into the next century. Perhaps the most stringent intellectual definition of crisis, for example, can be found in Godzich's argument that English studies (by which he clearly means literary studies) can no longer claim to be a discipline built on what he terms the "universal mediator" of human knowledge. Without this governing term, now provided largely by mathematics, Godzich claims, literary research can no longer command the sort of authority it wielded for much of the last century. This loss, Godzich believes, has its origins in both intellectual history and in the ongoing economic rationalizations of the global economy.

In contrast, Seitz's *Motives for Metaphor*, while it shares Godzich's focus on what I call an individualized, textual politics, differs sharply in how it conceives of the possibilities for reform. Seitz more realistically thinks of English studies as a discipline rooted in two quite distinct linguistic projects, if not epistemologies. Unlike Godzich, however, Seitz is less interested in reestablishing the perceived loss of status in literary studies. As a result, Seitz's program is more helpfully grounded in what he hopes will become a productive dialogue between rhetoric and composition and literary studies. Seitz and Godzich each illustrate the ways that the research-centered status system in English studies encourages a limited, discourse-oriented politics that seems wholly unaware of the wide variety of other modes of power—most important, those more related to collective organizing and service. Seitz, however, seems much more aware of local politics and of the specific agents of change.

In the terms I have developed in this book, Seitz is more alert to the political processes that define the composition of the professional cultural capital of English studies. Even more helpfully, the recent work of Miller and Parks seeks to facilitate change by turning academia's collective attention toward its own internal political and social processes. Among other things, for example, Miller argues against a too common belief in institutional determinism that leads to political fatalism. Similarly, using the example of the Conference on College Composition and Communication's 1974 declaration on "Students' Right to Their Own Language," Parks traces out the particular institutional and political mechanisms through which important political ideas are both absorbed and defanged. Each of these studies, I argue, represents a key demystification of politics in academia, a recognition that while complex and overdetermined, social systems are nonetheless human institutions capable of evolution, transformation, and change.

In the penultimate section of this chapter, I argue that while we may not come to any immediate, conclusive resolution to the problems that haunt English studies, we can at least agree that the institutional problems we face are by no means obscure. Put simply, English studies must begin to organize itself around a self-sustaining status system rooted in recognition of the importance of an autonomous intellectual culture. Along with James Sledd, I argue that this can be achieved only through unionization and subsequent democratization of the education system in the United States. Traditionally, English studies has been rooted in the recognition that society needed both free inquiry and debate and that education played a key role in class mobility and the maintenance of economic and social status. The linguistic epistemologies of English studies represented an attempt at balancing these sometimes contradictory desires and necessities. Yet these socioeconomic processes too often remain the dirty little secrets of an enterprise that cannot quite abandon its idealistic self-image. Unionization, I would argue, demands that English studies expand its traditional role in order to become a venue for the exploration and refinement of democratic self-management.

In concluding this chapter, and my study, I turn to Robert Birnbaum's discussion of what President John Adams once termed the "battle of the narratives." Essentially, Adams argued that education in a capitalist society is always intimately involved in class mobility and that as successive generations succeed, their needs and desires change. First generations, like my father's, demand practicality and in contemporary U.S. culture often focus on professional and business degrees. In Adams's terms, they focus on "politics" and necessity. The following generations of students, however, build on an economic and cultural base that allows them to broaden their aspirations into what Adams called the study of "porcelain." In other words, if, in my father's time, his education needed to focus on material capital, in my time I was able to widen my concerns to include cultural capital in a broad, inclusive sense. Briefly, I believe, this has been the trajectory of the U.S. middle class for much of the last century. If it is to continue, however, the system of status that underlies English studies, and indeed the entire educational enterprise, must be transformed into a self-governing, semi-autonomous democratic institution.

SISYPHUS IN TWEEDS

Wlad Godzich opens *The Culture of Literacy* by asking a simple question: Why has the perceived crisis in English studies resulted in calls for "a further instrumentalism of language" rather than "a greater appreciation of the multiplicity of functions that language performs" (5)? More mundanely, why has this crisis "set into motion a . . . redistribution of money and personnel away from the teaching of literature and criticism and towards the teaching of writing and composition" (1)? Godzich's explanation has two themes. First, literary criticism—or, more precisely, literary theory—has rejected wholesale the notion of language as a "universal mediator," a formulation that traditionally served as justification for its domination of English studies. "It has become impossible," Godzich writes, "to assert that language is a universal mediator: it can offer only rather gross and misleading approximations of what the physicists know through mathematical formulas" (11). Godzich, in contrast to Cleanth Brooks, would apparently admit defeat in English studies' long battle against a rigid scientific ideology.

Second, "powerful societal forces," Godzich argues gloomily, favor the "New Vocationalism," presumably in pursuit of their own commercial interests. Godzich includes in his critique advocates of the study of writing who have allied themselves with a "conservative determination to impose a core curriculum stressing so-called basics," a process that has occurred "at the expense of the regular English curriculum" (4). While Godzich understands this "crisis of literacy" against a milieu of media globalization and international corporate consolidation, he has little to say about who controls the university, much less the English department. If Godzich is correct about the detrimental effects of the current round of economic rationalization, and I believe he is, then surely academics have reason to begin to respond in an organized way. For Godzich, however, politics are never local, and we learn little—at least explicitly—about the ways in which the changes he has identified are taking shape in the institutions he tells us are rapidly re-tooling. Are department chairs and search committees abandoning literary faculty positions wholesale in order to hire new PhDs in rhetoric and composition? Are administrators imposing curricular reform that emphasizes a narrowly defined instrumental form of writing instruction?

Whatever the case, in Godzich's analysis, literacy has the same meaning and efficacy no matter what institution, professor, or student is under consideration. Godzich makes no inquiries about student needs or desires, and he appears wholly unaware of the realities of socioeconomic class. There seems to be no specific "subject" for whom "literacy" is in crisis. What broader economic forces might help explain a widespread student desire for the cultural capital Godzich finds so reprehensible? Are these same forces responsible for an administrative push for a vocationally focused curriculum? In the end, Godzich offers only an anecdote from intellectual history as an explanation for literary theory's inability to offer a rationale for its continued existence. Literary studies has failed to offer a positive alternative to the broader pressure toward fragmentation and vocational education, Godzich somewhat charitably contends,

> owing to the peculiar blindness that we share with respect to the nature of the historical process we inhabit, or indeed to the very notion that we inhabit a historical process. For this latter notion is typically Hegelian, and all American intellectuals have been brought up to believe that the specter of Hegelianism was successfully repulsed by William James shouting, "Damn the Absolute!" to Josiah Royce, a moment preserved in a famous Harvard photograph. (13)

Without Hegel, Godzich says—and his dialectic of Spirit that moves from thesis to antithesis to synthesis—literary criticism occupies a structural purgatory, unable to recognize history, much less to respond in kind.

What's more, Godzich continues, as some begin to argue that history is finally over, that Spirit has now reached full self-consciousness, theory sleeps. Interestingly, Godzich's story gently hints that the origin of this lack of historical understanding has deep roots in the ideologies of education and training that shape graduate school curricula. Academics ignore history, it might be argued, because they are trained to ignore history and because as tenured faculty it is in their professional interest to continue to do so. What this also suggests is that, if we are to "inhabit a historical process" relevant to our own professional preservation, we must make professionally viable a concern with teaching and service. Godzich offers little insight into why academia has traditionally ignored class, and his narrative seems wholly naive about education and socioeconomic mobility. Nevertheless, while English studies may well be in crisis, successful theorists continue to be well rewarded. Godzich's own class position, in other words, hardly seems threatened at all.

Outside the university, a multitude of agents contend for varying degrees of control over resources; inside, academics debate history, Godzich suggests, apparently uninvolved in the messy business of political maneuvering occurring just beyond the borders of campus. Yet as soon as this potentially productive hint is given voice, Godzich turns toward what he evidently feels is a much sexier object of desire, the solution to the dilemma of the ahistorical, or at least a strategy for academics interested in change. Given the betrayal of the instrumental compositionists and the loss of language as a universal mediator, what is to be done? Godzich offers his corrective, a "practice of resistance that is genuine theory" (33) and so "more akin to that of the refusenik, of the dissident, who rebels and resists but in a very subjective form of rebellion. A dissident is someone who denounces, and bears witness to, the abyss that separates reality from its official version. A dissident's stance draws attention to and inhabits this difference, letting it progressively inscribe itself in the dissident's very body" (31). Whatever the value of Godzich's work, it is hard not to see this position as almost unbearably romantic, a politics reduced down to the activities of the lone intellectual—Sisyphus in tweeds. It is also difficult not to hear in Godzich's grief a nostalgia for what in another context has been called the "apprenticeship model" of academia.

The reference to the former Soviet Union is in no sense a coincidence, either, since it reflects Godzich's collapse of ideology first into hegemony and then into deterministic authoritarianism. The processes of domination are the same for Godzich no matter what the specifics of the culture or class, much less gender or ethnicity; resisting the Communist Party in the 1970s is (nearly) identical to the processes of change in a democratic state in the 1990s. History is Hegelian history, it seems, in every time and place. Somewhat less charitably, I might offer a more transparent explanation for theory's ongoing lack of engagement in change: that the current system of cultural capital within English studies rewards research over teaching and service and so encourages a politics of what can be called discursive performance. Status (and often tenure) is earned in English studies not by negotiating a series of successful union contracts but by publishing texts. Perhaps theory is no longer the darling of academia, but the investment of time and energy it represents still reaps rich social and economic rewards for the so-called academic celebrities.

Ironically, in Godzich's narrative, the ongoing reproduction and successful investment of academic cultural capital continues unabated, despite or perhaps because of economic globalization. When Godzich speaks of dissidence and of resistance, finally, he is not referring to the years of mundane work—meetings, rallies, position papers, and the like—that are a prelude to the success of a reform movement. Instead, what Godzich seems to be referring to is an intellectual attitude embodied in a form of writing that, whatever its merits, has little hope of achieving the kinds of goals that by definition must be accomplished by other means. Godzich's subtle rhetoric of self-interest is, unfortunately, more common than it might seem at first glance. More recently, for example, Seitz's *Motives for Metaphor* reproduces Godzich's focus on attitudes and texts, even if his analysis differs in its formulations of responsibility and suggestions for reform.

Seitz is speaking from a position of relative authority carved out by compositionists in the years since the early 1990s, when Godzich published *The Culture of Literacy*, but his description of his own employment situation, toward the end of his prologue, reminds us that his program has familiar borders:

> I normally teach four courses per academic year, two of which are designated by the department in which I teach and by the campus course directory as "literature" courses (one introductory and one advanced or graduate level), while the other two are designated as "composition" courses (one freshman and one advanced). I also receive two courses of release time from the department's "three-three" teaching load for research, writing, and administrative or committee work. (18)

Readers teaching in comprehensive institutions with four-four teaching loads and little or no release time may feel a bit of justifiable envy at Seitz's situation; those in the junior colleges with five-fives could not be criticized for their anger. "My teaching situation is not simply comfortable;" Seitz admits; "it is in many ways ideal" (18).

In any case, Seitz has a very different take on the relationship between literary studies and theory and rhetoric and composition: "Yet, strangely enough, at the same time that it looks as if composition and literary studies have in many respects continued to move their separate ways, they may now have more pressing reasons for working together than members of either field seem to recognize" (19). Gone from this account is composition's surrender to vocation and objectivity and betrayal of the higher aspirations of literature; gone too is the implication that literature and theory must once again take up their historic roles of leadership in the department. Seitz is careful to avoid blame, an understandable move in any call for solidarity among colleagues, dissidents or otherwise. Given the kind of institution Seitz works in, we might suppose him less predisposed to dismiss the more utilitarian and vocational demands of his students. Unlike in Godzich's situation, Seitz's students would have been less likely to come to the university with the cultural capital represented by the freshman English course. Yet Seitz is invested as much in the field of literature as in composition.

Seitz also echoes Godzich's concern that it is the literary rather than the composition specialist whose job may be in peril:

> After all, if administrators, state legislatures, corporations, parents, and students themselves come to demand (as many already do) that a college education primarily provide the "basic skills" imagined necessary for employment, then teaching positions in the upper end of the curriculum will be those deemed most expendable (as some English departments have already discovered). (20)

In contrast to Godzich, Seitz portrays the loss of literary resources as an unrealized potential; he speaks of "upper level courses" rather than the "regular English curriculum"; and he emphasizes that in the end, compositionists have little to gain from literature's losses. Yet when Seitz outlines the details of his plan, the differences between his work and Godzich's recede sharply. Here, too, textual performance rather than social organization is the preferred political mode.

PROFESSING CULTURAL CAPITAL

Seitz's apprehension about the future of English studies, like Godzich's, is primarily attitudinal and curricular, focused on the creation of a departmental agenda that, in Gerald Graff's famous phrase, "teaches the conflicts": "If those of us working in the broad field of English are to reimagine the structure and functions of our discipline and the relationships we cultivate, then it may be useful to discuss the possibility of a curriculum, not just a theory, in which writing and teaching are valued precisely because of the ways they place their own procedures into doubt" (20). Nonetheless, Seitz seems well aware of the institutional and cultural contexts in which the nominal crisis is occurring. Instead of the hazy but menacing threat of "powerful social forces" and globalization, Seitz's list of actors is refreshingly concrete: "administrators, state legislatures, corporations, parents, and students." And Seitz is both more accurate when it comes to the current distribution of resources in English departments, generally speaking, and more valuable in his notion of metaphor as a stepping stone to intellectual peace in English studies. He thus addresses a set of problems that Godzich simply ignores. Seitz also offers a very workable alternative to the loss of a "universal mediator" in his notion of metaphor as the connective tissue of English studies. Seitz's thinking about the process of reform, in other words, is tied to social relationships and so, implicitly, to the ongoing struggles over the composition of cultural capital in our field.

Seitz's argument additionally contends with the system that underlies the professional status of English professors, suggesting that teaching as well as research should be rewarded professionally. Yet Seitz stops short when it comes to a discussion of what academics must do if they are to face up to the pressures asserted from his catalog of interest groups; instead of organizing a countervailing organizational and institutional force, Seitz wants more internal dialogue. "In the years to come," Seitz writes, "the capacity for forging some such alliance [between disciplines of English studies] may determine whether the study of reading and writing continues to be regarded as necessary merely for the sake of 'functioning' in society, or whether it becomes something else altogether: a sphere for the investigation, re-creation, and critique of metaphor, of literalism, of language itself" (205).

It in no way minimizes Seitz's efforts to note that by "alliance" he is referring to formal intellectual discussions (the discursive systems of conferences and journals) rather than to the forms of self-organization associated with the professoriat at the departmental or university level. Here, as in Godzich, the project of reform is primarily a task of persuasion, a matter of the creation of consensus among so-called discourse communities, and not changes in our systems of promotion and reward or differing forms of social organization. In Godzich, the social processes of the formation of cultural capital remain reified. Understandably, perhaps, Seitz wants the literature professors to grant their composition colleagues the right to earn their status in the traditional way: through research.

In contrast, Miller opens *As If Learning Mattered* with a frankly critical admission about the traditional academic culture in which he works: "One need only point to the long and venerable tradition of declaring one educational crisis after another to see that willed ignorance about the bureaucratic intricacies of life in the academy is often understood to be both a virtue and a sign of elevated intelligence" (3). Miller wishes to shift our attention away from what he feels is a culturally shaped notion of deterministic fatalism—the academy as "total institution"—and toward a more grounded politics in which our own practices are examined in hopes of furthering change. In institutions such as the army or prison, Miller writes, "the hierarchal relations among members are rigorously policed and each member's actions are subject to continuous and potentially endless review" (3). What makes the university different, Miller argues, is the relative autonomy of the professors. In such an institution, Miller reminds us, "there are other, more productive ways of responding . . . than sinking into ironic detachment" (3). Our autonomy, in other words, allows for a certain freedom that is often ignored. Miller wishes to reallocate our energy away from the theoretical debates over "politically charged subject matter" and toward a greater understanding of how these ideas are integrated into the work of teachers and students (3).

Similarly, Parks begins his historical analysis of the Conference on College Composition and Communication's 1974 declaration on "Students' Right to Their Own Language" with the thesis that the professionalization of composition has been accompanied by a rejection of "interdisciplinary and interorganizational movements for political change" as "the type of academic and organizational behavior that true professionalism has rejected" (3). Parks suggests that hitherto unacknowledged work in service, particularly in the professional organizations of academia, has had a decisive effect on the way that the political debates always going on in society at large are defanged as they are incorporated into the academy. These two studies represent a new, and I believe more productive, turn in the long debate over the future of English studies, locating the source of our continuing troubles not solely in hegemonic ideology but in the specifics of the classroom, the department, and the university. In Pierre Bourdieu's terms, each of these studies represents an investigation into the cultural capital of English studies as an ongoing historical process, here represented not as a given set of values but as a series of negotiations and exchanges shaping the accumulation of professional cultural capital.

Miller recognizes both the constraints of the bureaucratized university—the inertia of academic cultural capital—and what he calls "slippage," a tendency of such institutions to fail to act as expected. As such, Miller says, academic practices are best defined as "a series of complex, contradictory, compromised, and contingent solutions whose permanence is never assumed" (8). Miller concludes that this way of understanding the crisis allows us to "move on to a consideration of what has been thought possible under the less-than-ideal conditions educators have faced, where there has been and always will be a slippage between the worlds that can be created in words, and the worlds lived in by real people" (9). While I might not fully accept Miller's slight hyperbole—the "always" he identifies as a by-product of language, presumably always and everywhere—I find it difficult to fault his reasoning. Ideology, as a political process in a democratic society, is in some sense always a matter of interaction among agents, even if we acknowledge that these actors are not always or even often equal antagonists.

Among the most important factors shaping these labor practices are the interrelationships among the values assigned to research, teaching, and service that drive status in the academy. The internal system by which we distribute resources is in turn shaped by the ongoing disciplinary debates, which have so far dominated discussions over the future of English studies. Too often, these debates suffer from an unrealistically heavy emphasis on the discursive practices of the university. The pen, in other words, is the only source of power. Yet, as Parks's analysis makes clear, these contentions occur within a context of professionalization, a process of "building professional knowledge . . . that negates much of their efficacy" as reform (250). Here, too, our attention is drawn away from the outside world and toward the assumptions and processes that shape our professional lives. Together, Parks and Miller represent what might be called a Pogo moment in academia: We have met the enemy and he is us. Alternatively, rather, the enemy is less a particular metaphysical or pragmatic stance toward language than the institutional system through which we grant status.

This is not to argue, of course, in favor of social isolation but to say that we have to begin to challenge the "insulation" that has become "insularity." "The historical impulses of the SRTOL [Students' Right to Their Own Language]," Parks writes,

> are not properly the sole domain of the CCCC [or of the] NCTE [National Council of Teachers of English]. Instead . . . a new organization is needed which will work to bring together progressive caucuses and community organizations committed to the expansion of critical democracy. Such an alliance would be concerned not just with the production of disciplinary knowledge . . . but with connecting such knowledge to practical community work. (250)

In Parks's vision of English studies, a recognition of the myriad actors implicated in an issue, both as personal and as socially important as language, necessitates the formation of alliances outside of academia. In my terms, the weight of our own cultural capital, the authority we bring to discussions of education and language, would be counterbalanced through an ongoing engagement with groups whose authority has very different sources of reproduction and maintenance. Here, "writing in the wild" pedagogy finds an institutional analogy. Put another way, what we imagine in research must be informed by service as well as by teaching. Parks's strategy both recognizes the value of specialization and offers a corrective to its inherent problems. Instead of a product in the form of a disciplinary definition or a self-evident justification, Parks, like Miller, offers a political process. This strategy, I can't help but add, is one that is well outside of the traditional avenues of publication and status.

The limitations to Parks's scheme as the foundation of the beginning of a substantive reform movement lie not so much in the lack of individual desire or collective will as they do in the "local labor practices" through which we work. A sustained challenge to the power of the English department involves an investment of time and energy risky for most probationary faculty or perhaps professionally suicidal for the part-time and adjunct faculty who more and more dominate our field. Put still another way, Parks's analysis suggests what might well already be obvious: that graduate students, facing the roulette wheel of a job market, have the least to lose from the creation of a professional system less rooted in publication and research and more grounded in the democratic sociality of the labor union. There are structural reasons, in short, for the current leadership status of our PhD candidates in unionization, as well for the problems created by our predisposition to embrace the authority of a status system centered on research.

Miller's and Parks's respective projects begin to suggest a viable alternative to what Stephen M. North has called our three options of "dissolution, corporate compromise, and fusion" (253). In fact, there is no reason that North's preferred solution of "fusion" could not proceed quite successfully alongside an effective project of reform. Professors of English studies may well be less predisposed then to the more destructive forms of self-interest North portrays and so more willing to devote a larger proportion of their energies to service and teaching. Clearly, however, only a change in our institutional priorities can ensure that such activities are rescued from the margins of academia. Influence, however powerful, is not control, and within that slippage we could begin to create a system in which publication, research, and service to the profession and to students are equally rewarded. Such a system would be no less "complex, contradictory, compromised, and contingent," but it would have the advantage of moving us past our current sense of crisis and into a productive and creative relationship with the world in which the school is embedded. It is that relationship, I would argue, that creates—or can re-create, in many cases—our own sense of legitimate work in English studies.

Most important, it would ally us much more closely with the historical projects of class mobility and democratic transformation, balancing our autonomy against our responsibility to the greater good. Disciplinary fusion rests on the apparent assumption that the difference between composition and literature is an arbitrary artifact of our professional history rather than a negotiated response to emerging social and economic conditions. Even in a world in which all students were well served from preschool to high school, the university would need to be concerned with a communicative ethos. Assuming that the distinction can simply be set aside is an intellectual gambit that risks ignoring what I have called the differing efficacies of the cultural capital represented by each area of expertise. Again, it suggests a solution that ignores the constraints of the lived world, particularly when it comes to the ongoing dynamics of class. That is, we too must negotiate our own response in light of currently emerging conditions rather than simply create a solution in writing.

As I have outlined in the case of my father, composition and literature arguably represent very different sorts of desires and needs that can, in part, be traced back to the dynamics of education and class mobility in the culture at large. The habitus imagined by English studies is both pragmatic and utopian. The question of the relationship between composition and literature is sociological as well as disciplinary; it is about a taste for language. These dynamics are further complicated by the distributions of resources along hierarchal lines in the educational system at large. Here, too, the problem we face is hidden quite out in the open: we cannot equate the needs of an inner-city student with those of the privileged sons and daughters of the Ivy League. Even if we were to define the purposes of education in the broadest possible way, as one of the key means of gaining access to knowledge and culture, as I believe we should, how we get there is by no means self-evident.

THE HIERARCHY AT LARGE

The hierarchy of the formalist aesthetic over the popular ethos in academia has effects well beyond the individual writer or the isolated institution. Arguably, it has had a profound effect on the way the U.S. education system is organized, broadly speaking. Writing of the efforts at reform at the State University of New York–Albany, North notes that, whatever its successes, "Albany is not Harvard or Yale, Stanford or Wisconsin, Columbia or Princeton; it does not . . . bring to the table . . . the cumulative institutional momentum and resources that, in U.S. higher education, tend to accrue thereto" (xvi). The limits to the sorts of reformist impulses noted by North have institutional and historical roots too often unacknowledged in discussions of our intellectual pedigrees and our professional futures. To paraphrase Bourdieu, the greater the distance from necessity, the more abstract and "pure" the research, the more status accrues. Why shouldn't Albany be able to provide leadership in curricular reform? Perhaps more important, why does Princeton command so much power? The obviousness of the answers ought not to obscure the necessity of challenging these forms of power.

At the most general level, a status system so heavily invested in textual performance depletes service and teaching as alternative avenues of ongoing reform. This concentration of resources in research is the result of a historical process of accumulation at the institutional level, and, as Bourdieu has emphasized, any such capital has an inherent inertia, a powerful tendency to continue in its current form. It's not hard to imagine the thoughts of an older faculty member when faced with the prospect of younger colleagues who no longer earn tenure largely through publication. What would be the equivalent investment in time and energy to publishing two books? How can the values of research be made equivalent to the values of service and teaching? What would be the exchange rate? What might be the thoughts of a professor of comparative literature at the University of Pennsylvania when he or she is told that departmental reform will be modeled on a design originating at a state college in California? As difficult as these questions may be, and I think their difficulty cannot be overstated, they are precisely the questions we must ask if we are to consider reform and to attend to contemporary changes in the U.S. education system.

At bottom, the uneasiness of the alliance of composition and literary studies is rooted in the nominal contradictions between the popular ethos and the formalist aesthetic and between a notion of language as pragmatic tool and one that emphasizes aesthetics and form. This tension between instrumentalism and art continues to shape English studies. Evan Watkins offers one species of this conflict as it has emerged in debates over popular culture:

> "Popular culture," it is asserted, touches the entire range of the population in one way or the other, and we may thereby expect to find articulated within it, in however disguised forms, the authentic hopes and desires of the people, as opposed to "high" art whose complexities, whose locus of production and consumption in the university, and whose blatant disregard for what the "ordinary" person could possibly understand mark it as an elitist defense of intellectual privilege. (67)

Here, "popular culture" is held up as a transparent medium through which "authentic desires" are unproblematically articulated, and "high art" is figured as the realm of experts, an opaque, difficult expression that "the people" need help to understand (67). This same conflict, Watkins says, can also be described in quite the opposite way:

> Alternately, "popular art" is understood to be a reflex of commodity structure, a reification of the aesthetic such that the only "end" of cultural production becomes the endless consumption of images that drug the masses, a spectacle that as "leisure time" at once reproduces and compensates for their exploited labor. "High" art in its very complexity resists assimilation and is thereby able to maintain an authentic and subversive stance, increasingly the sole remaining place of the "negative" to challenge the positive and persuasive force of a culture industry. (67)

In a similar way, I would describe the academic and intellectual conflicts between the popular ethos and the formalist aesthetics as a debate between competing forms of social elitism and populism.

Historically, as I have noted, this presumed predominance of literature and research has its roots in reform efforts associated with the Progressive Era; the institutional system of professional carrots and sticks developed in that context is what I would argue must now be challenged. Silence on the memoranda and the position paper and on the power they can represent reflects a deeper unease about class and about the cultural capital—the competencies and skills—represented by these forms of writing. As academia fumes over vocational pedagogy, technology, and the job market, the need for some understanding of these quotidian forms of literacy grows. In this sense, arguments over rhetoric and composition and literature are in fact contentions about our own relatively privileged status as professors. The era of the progressive movement transformed academia, institutionalizing tenure and academic freedom of speech and laying the groundwork for our current system of professional schools, among many other things. The GI Bill set the stage for decades of growth in the academic job market, helping to ensure that PhDs, schooled in literature and earning their way as composition instructors, would find secure jobs on graduation. Sledd has summarized this more recent history succinctly: "While the prosperity lasted, English departments—at least their literary components—prospered too. As access to higher education opened, more students in the new or growing colleges and universities took BAs in English; and from 1960 almost to 1970, the swarm of new PhDs found, happily, that there were more jobs than candidates" (12). The heart of this system was the recognition of society's vested interest in free inquiry on the one hand and in class mobility on the other. As Sledd notes, the linchpins of this system began to change in the late 1960s; tenure-track positions, particularly in literature, dried up, and the use of adjunct labor grew exponentially. As tuition rose and affirmative action declined, tenure began to be challenged, particularly in relation to teaching effectiveness. Meanwhile, the public schools faced privatization, budget cuts directed at the arts, attacks on teachers' unions, and an increasing reliance on standardized tests.

Yet, even after more than a decade of often-bitter contention over these issues and of social and economic changes that are as dramatic as those of the early years of the twentieth century, our era has produced progressive academic voices but not a broad-based reform movement for educational reform. Given the political nature of the debate, why haven't those in the professoriat organized themselves into a national movement? Any answer to that admittedly complex question has to begin with a simple fact, hidden in plain sight: no one gets tenure for helping to negotiate a union contract or for serving on the board of directors of a university as a faculty representative. We reward publication, not activism. That obvious truth has tended to obscure the myriad effects of the tripartite system of capital under which we all work: research, service, and teaching. Indeed, even the ordering of my list is the start of an analysis of status among the academic cadres: putting research first suggests the highest tiers of the university hierarchy; putting it last, that of the lowest.

Beyond that recognition, it has to be acknowledged that the debate over the future of English studies is predisposed toward writers in research universities, and so in some sense toward academics who work in these sorts of institutions and the students who study there. At research institutions, the pressure toward a politics of discursive performance is particularly acute. With certain exceptions, whatever else these writers have to say about the aims and goals of English, they are largely silent on the different forms of cultural capital that students and professors bring to the classroom. Yet too often, we speak as if they were the same species, in effect ignoring the complex ramifications of the unequal distribution of capital characteristic of the U.S. economy. Accumulation matters for teachers as well as for students, and it cannot be forgotten that the writers most often heard, or heard most insistently, in the debate over English studies have the most invested in the current system.

POLITICS AND PORCELAIN

In outlining the modern history of composition, Sledd goes on to argue that professional self-interest, rather than institutional reform, has governed the new discipline of rhetoric and composition, a desire for what he calls "upward mobility for a minority of lower managers" (12). Sledd further contends—persuasively, in my view—that the current system of academic rank ought to be abolished and that the energy now expended arguing about disciplinary boundaries could be better spent "in militant, inclusive unions—unions of both faculty and staff, all as workers together, not underlings and upperlings" (28). Sledd also argues that tenure, as now constituted, too often cannot protect freedom of speech: "Administrators have lots of ways of controlling the tenured: denial of raises, punitive course assignments, banishment from faculty councils and significant committees, post-tenure review (recently installed at the University of Texas), early retirement, covert censorship of the media, speech with forked tongue" (26). In Sledd's view, any attempts at reform must begin with a broad-based coalition, uniting not simply the separate faculties of English studies but also the rest of the academic community—exclusive of administrative management, presumably, above the level of departmental chair. Given the magnitude of the forces I have listed and the many fronts on which the autonomy of the university has been challenged, solidarity of the sort suggested by Sledd seems the only effective answer. Capital, of course, has a myriad of organizational forms designed to serve its self-interest; as always, labor has no choice but to do likewise.

The greatest challenge to solidarity within English departments, as Sledd emphasizes, is the hierarchy of the assistant, associate, and full professor. A democratic university does not mean full autonomy; as Sledd says, "Society pays us, and rightly so, for learning and teaching. The next question follows: For what learning and what teaching?" (27). This goal of a democratically (re)organized university system in no way suggests that academia abandon its historical commitments to the greater social good; protecting our own material and social interests need not preclude a notion of service to society broadly conceived. As Sledd writes, there is "plenty of time and room for research and argument about such things," and our first priority ought to be organizing around the goal of strengthening our institution (27). Once "the whole stupid professional hierarchy [comes] tumbling down" under a unionized university, Sledd argues, courses would be assigned,

> not according to position on the totem pole, but according to ability to teach them. New appointees might be assigned to graduate courses, pompous veterans to teach freshmen; and if either group flubbed its assignment, the flubbers would be offered re-training, then (if all else failed) a quiet dismissal. All teachers would work along a uniform pay scale, with automatic raises for seniority as long as performance remained satisfactory. (26–27)

Although Sledd doesn't make this point clearly, it is important to note that the criteria of these assessments would have to be subject to negotiations both within and without the department and beyond. Such an arrangement would tend to undermine narrow specialization, encouraging work that crosses disciplines and subdisciplines, since academics would no longer be competing against each other for coveted positions higher in the hierarchy.

In the current system, Sledd writes, "clawing for tenure in a savage competition, the upwardly mobile learn subservience to superiors. Most (not all) tenured academics have studied to be mouselike, to squeak at command or hole up" (26). A unionized and restructured university system, then, would encourage intellectual and social independence as well as interdependence and would protect academic freedom of speech by allowing all workers at a university to participate in the governance of their own workplace. Even under a democratic system, of course, professional competition would continue, if on a new, more secure institutional basis. Internally, English studies would still have to determine, however independently, how to distribute resources—time and energy—among its various tasks. A democratic university, then, would also have to include among its goals a commitment to modify the relationships among research, service, and teaching that undergird the profession of English professor.

Sledd argues, in this context, for "a return to service" in composition, a renewed commitment to both the university as such and to society at large. "In the democratic university of my imagining," Sledd says acerbically, "the whole faculty would walk out and close the place down if the football coach got a million a year while TAs survived on a pittance and librarians qualified for food stamps" (28). Like Sledd, I believe that what is most needed today is not more debate over professionalization in composition but a clear recognition that "the pre-requisite for all successful education . . . is decent working conditions for teachers and learners" (27). Arguably, if we do not reorganize the department and the university in support of academic freedom of speech and autonomy, it will be done for us in support of the hegemony of the capitalist economy. Indeed, this reorganization against our autonomy is already well underway.

Sledd's argument can be usefully extended with a finer understanding of how the cultural capital of English studies has shaped our intellectual traditions, particularly when it comes to the values we place on our own writing.

> Twenty years ago a big survey at the University of Texas at Austin made it clear what kinds of writing un-English faculty wanted from their students. They wanted clarity of statement, intelligible organization, reasonably justified assertions, mechanical and grammatical correctness—in other words, the sort of general purpose prose that one reads in the minutes of faculty meetings, in respectable journals, or in the arguments of denigrators of general-purpose prose. (27)

Sledd advocates a continued focus in composition on the refinement of the popular ethos. In order to understand the system of capital under which we operate, however, it is also necessary to understand how this ethos works both with and against aesthetics. What Sledd (perhaps purposely) understates in his polemic against current trends in composition, in other words, is that literary academics espouse a quite different epistemology of language. The hierarchies of aesthetic over popular ethos have to be challenged along with that of rank and status.

Robert Birnbaum, quoting John Adams, has helpfully provided a summary of the role of academic leadership in an era in which many feel that universities have lost their way:

> In a letter to his wife . . . Adams proposed that education for a democracy might pass through three developmental stages. He wrote, "I must study politics and war that my sons may have liberty to study mathematics and philosophy. My sons ought to study mathematics and philosophy, geography, natural history, naval architecture, navigation, commerce and agriculture, in order to give their children a right to study painting, poetry, music, architecture, statuary, tapestry, and porcelain." We have been exceptionally successful in exploiting this second developmental stage, but we appear increasingly reluctant to make the evolutionary advance from studying politics to studying porcelain. (19)

In my own case, it can be said that my father studied "politics and war" so that I could study "mathematics and philosophy." To stretch the analogy, my father went to college to accumulate enough economic capital so that his children could then attend a university in pursuit of economic as well as cultural capital. Fully middle-class economically, my children, nieces, and nephews could then, potentially, embrace their "right to study painting, poetry, music, architecture, statuary, tapestry, and porcelain." If in my father's time, in other words, education had reason to be largely vocational, the very successes of education means that it can today become something more; the middle classes now have the leverage they need to extend democratic culture beyond necessity. The pragmatic institutional arrangements represented by traditional English studies have outlived their usefulness, both as disciplinary justifications and as systems of hierarchical status.

Universities, Birnbaum argues, are losing the "battle of the narratives," the master stories that help to explain their purposes and goals:

> The educational narratives of the past have been stories of personal virtues, civic participation, democracy, and social equality. The narrative . . . of the present appear[s] to be economic utility, consumerism and technology—weak foundations on which to build a just social order. . . . Our past narratives spoke to a liberating education, to critical thinking, to full involvement in citizenship, to personal growth, and to social justice. (18)

Technology, for example, is too often presented as a kind of quick fix to the perceived problems of higher education. "It has led to huge expenditures of money and effort," Birnbaum writes, "while experts continue to question whether any data indicate that the goals of lower cost and higher quality have been—or can be—met" (19). In addition, and most important, many feel that universities must adopt "the new management techniques believed to be successful in business." As I have argued, this process has deep historical roots in the progressive era of institutional reform. Yet, Birnbaum writes, universities are not "a convenience store where isolated and disembodied individuals measure out virtual units of teaching or learning" (19). In Evan Watkins's terms, the university is neither a factory nor a linguistic-consultant service agency. For Birnbaum, the substantive danger facing universities today is that if "we are seen as being no different than business then we can be . . . judged by business standards" (19). What universities must do, Birnbaum believes, is to begin to articulate an agenda distinct if not separate from the realms of economy and business.

How might we launch "the evolutionary advance from studying politics to studying porcelain"? As Birnbaum suggests, I believe that we must return to those "narratives" of a "liberating education" that in our own time could provide a rationale for "critical thinking, . . . full involvement in citizenship, . . . personal growth, and . . . social justice." As a pragmatic response, I believe we can best launch this development of a distinct agenda by first setting aside the epistemological dilemmas of language as foundational ideologies in the discipline of English studies. Indeed, our strength is in our pragmatic endorsement of a seeming contradiction between ethos and aesthetic, adaptation and vision. Composition instructors may well always debate the question of whether or not what I have called the popular ethos is an ideological manipulation or simply a matter of accessibility. Similarly, argument on the metaphysical implications of the formalist aesthetic and literature is not likely to subside quickly. Ideas of language and identity, moreover, as Cleanth Brooks emphasized, are hypothetical propositions more than fixed answers. Consensus on these linguistic issues seems unlikely. It is possible, however, that we might begin to see our divisiveness as vitality, our divisions as reflections of the importance and complexity of language and education in a democratic society.

THE BATTLE OF THE NARRATIVES

Even if we never fully resolve the metaphysical questions that have haunted our profession, I believe we can come to some tentative conclusions about the sorts of practices and institutions that we desire, given the society we know and the future we want. Its first principle would be that all teachers deserve and need self-governing unions through which they can protect their professional interests. At the disciplinary center of English studies would be a revived and re-envisioned alliance between ethos and aesthetics, one founded in recognition of the subtle dynamics that link these differing ways of understanding and using language. The traditional hierarchy of English studies helped to support both exploitation and a degradation of an education in the English language. A revised English studies, then, would start with a set of pragmatic principles about the study of language and literature in a capitalist economy. Certainly, we can all agree that our students must eventually earn a living. To some extent, moreover, their successful employment is dependent on an ethos that emphasizes concise, clear language.

Again, few would argue that everyday communication—even everyday professional communication in English departments—ought to fully embrace a formalist aesthetic as its model. Students need to learn a popular ethos that emphasizes audiences and communication. I also suspect that few academics would disagree with the notion that we want our students to learn to see their lives as broader in scope than the horizons of their professional tasks. Indeed, arguably, few of our students need to be reminded that the market too often circumscribes their lives; if nothing else, the ongoing rise in the cost of tuition and textbooks serves as a reminder of this fact. Also, I think few academics would disagree with the notion that while utility is important, so is beauty and contemplation. In terms of writing, this means we need memos that are easy to understand, but we also need poetry, even if it is at times a struggle to comprehend. I would argue that we should consider the importance of beauty in technical writing, too. Our pedagogical agenda can start, then, with a pragmatic understanding of the variety of purposes that language can serve and with our desire to engage students in an active exploration of the ethos as well as of the aesthetics of writing. With Ralph Waldo Emerson, we can "gather from far every ray of various genius" to our too often inhospitable halls ("American Scholar" 12). This project cannot be politically naive, however, even if its utopian and prophetic bent stands in stark opposition to the current political climate.[1]

In the "battle of the narratives," our project must be a return to English studies' traditional project of enabling class mobility. In this sense, our unionized campuses will become one of our most important ongoing commentaries on the society in which we live. The story we need to tell is not simply a tale about the importance of studying language but also a narrative of the importance of institutional autonomy and democratic organization. Democracies need universities, and they need independent intellectuals free to investigate language and writing as they see fit. That independence cannot be guaranteed via discourse alone. The breakup of philology had ill effects politically as well as intellectually, helping to ensure that English studies would create English departments divided between haves and have-nots. Any attempt at reform has to be rooted in a system of cultural capital in which service, teaching, and research have equivalent roles. Similarly, English studies must incorporate its own insights into the limits of objectivity and positivism into its institutional practices, particularly the system of rewards and sanctions that underwrite academic freedom of speech and tenure.

If the popular ethos needs the formalist aesthetic, it must also be acknowledged that art cannot escape quotidian reality. Crucial concerns in this context are ongoing debates about the variety of evaluations educators perform, from standardized testing in the public schools to university admissions policies. In these debates, we help to determine the value of the linguistic cultural capital our students accumulate. The alliance of composition and literary studies, I would argue, has a vital stake in the outcome of these controversies and in developing non-positivist assessment methods, in both employment and classroom assessment. Here, too, unionization can help to ensure that standards and rubrics are developed through transparent debate rather than are imposed from the top down. Traditional forms of assessment are, in many ways, the last positivist holdouts in American intellectual life. Reductionist assessment contradicts the most basic insights of both composition and literary studies, our shared recognition of the uses and the limits of language. A communicative ethos isn't simple and cannot be collapsed into grammatical fidelity;

the inculcation of an aesthetic cannot be captured in the snapshots of essay exams, much less standardized tests.

Less familiar issues related to the organization of English departments are equally important. Along with our pragmatics of language, for example, I believe English studies is in need of a political narrative that defines an ethics of labor policy in universities. Just as we teach collaboration, we need to organize in support of our interests and in the interest of promoting our educational ideals. Our labor policies and democratic organization can serve as a model for just compensation for effective work analogous to the more narrowly defined ideal of the prevailing wage. Here lies one of our most important and least acknowledged powers in creating a better society. The lesser status of composition instruction has played a central but deleterious role in the history of English studies. Composition has come a long way toward gaining full academic respectability, but in our time, the ongoing reliance on part-time labor, graduate students, and adjuncts has reasserted and reinforced the worst features of the "grim apprenticeship." To the extent that we accept exploitation of labor in our own departments, we promote it in the culture at large.

Much more is at stake in contemporary university employment policies, which have helped to create the ongoing job crisis faced by PhDs. If the finances of English studies are not a zero-sum game—and I would contend that they are not—the newly unionized department and university would need to direct much of its considerable energy and power toward the creation of more full-time positions in both literature and composition. On the one hand, this would mean the creation of departments made up equally of PhDs trained in literary programs and PhDs trained in composition programs. We must move toward flattening the educational hierarchies as well; class sizes and workloads should be no higher at comprehensive universities than at research institutions; smaller writing classes are more effective at every level of the educational hierarchy. Specialization is more than simply an institutional convenience; it's a reflection of desire expressed through avocation. I have no wish to spend my days reading medieval manuscripts, but

I respect those who do. Teaching writing may often be vocational, but I may also wish to pursue research without any apparent practical end. We cannot abandon the ideal of "research for its own sake" without also abandoning our autonomy.

On the other hand, whatever the degrees of specialization, every program needs to include the popular ethos as well as the formalist aesthetic in its curricula. Even if a student wishes to spend her time teaching the ins and outs of language as a professor of literature, she still needs to know the ways and means of effective communication, particularly in the service of her profession and her students. Indeed, our very institutional survival depends on these abilities. Our other options in this crisis, I would argue, are severely limited. If we simply shrink the numbers of students admitted to graduate programs of any kind, we risk an eventual shortage of teachers. If we rely on part-time positions and adjuncts, we threaten intellectual freedom. A two-tiered system of a few well-paid and independent literary teachers and researchers working side-by-side with poorly compensated part-time composition teachers would hardly support the interests of our profession, our students, or our society. There are no theoretical limits to the use of adjunct labor—indeed, we could as easily imagine specialists in ethos becoming the haves and aesthetics delegated to part-timers. To be credible as academic leaders, in short, we must get our own house in order. Whatever our strategies in the face of these problems of abstract labor, the availability of economic resources needed for their resolution depends largely on our ability to articulate a coherent cultural purpose for the study of English language and literature. Again, we simply will not have the influence we need to shape that process without unionization.

If the purpose of our concrete labor in language is to be more widely persuasive, it must be firmly rooted in the traditions of democracy and education in the United States. Central to those traditions, as I have shown through my father's story, is the idea that a university degree is a route to a better life. As I have argued, class mobility cannot be reduced to either financial or existential status, nor can it be collapsed into either a mechanical reproduction of hegemony or a realm of essential freedom. At midcentury, students like my father went to institutions like LSU to escape poverty, and as I hope is clear, in these terms the results were necessarily mixed: in some ways, my father became middle-class, and in some ways he did not, either by choice or necessity. Some might contend that today the majority of students desire not to transform but to maintain their status as members of the middle class. Clearly, if we do not begin to confront the dominance of economics over democracy, we will increasingly find only the most middle-class students in our classroom. In either case, I would argue, our renewed sense of direction should acknowledge that economic status and class is a question of taste and sensibilities as well as of financial status and jobs. This recognition, and the corresponding respect for vocation, need not be simply dystopian; indeed, it suggests a utopian vision of a society both ethically sound and beautiful. In order to articulate this agenda of transformation and continuance, we particularly need to know much more about the inculcation of linguistic aesthetics in the classroom and its social and economic efficacy in the U.S. setting. One aim of a literary pedagogy, as Guillory has argued, must be to ensure the widest possible availability of the cultural capital represented by the formalist aesthetic and so neutralize its "elitist" rarity as a form of cultural capital.

Similarly, composition studies might refocus its already fruitful investigation of the refinement of the popular ethos in the classroom toward a fuller understanding of cultural capital and class as such. The relationships between popular ethos and aesthetics would necessarily play an important role in this examination. In my view, ethnographic methodology—that is, a research model consisting of a combination of textual analysis, interviews, and on-site observations of writers—is ideally suited to the pursuit of these aims, in both literary- and composition-based classrooms. Without some sort of ethnographic counterpoint, the library-based model of the research paper can only encourage students in their belief that communication is a simple matter of adherence to rules and that aesthetics is unimportant outside of school. Ethnographic case studies can help socialize the epistemological naturalism of the school by asking students to investigate how linguistic cultural capital is invested "in the wild." That is, rather than attempt to prescriptively instruct students about what their linguistic cultural capital ought to be, we could ask them to critically investigate the use of language in quotidian life. Here, I believe, we can begin to develop a body of persuasive research and opinion that would support our view of language and our desires for society. Literary studies, in this sense, must follow the lead of rhetoric and composition and seek its justification outside of the classroom and the rarified realm of art.

Equally important is an articulation of the differing efficacy of each linguistic competence and an investigation of how the sequence of courses affects the successful mastery of each. The conventional order of courses, first composition and then literature, may simply reinforce a student's sense that the popular ethos is more important than the formalist aesthetic. Given that the formalist aesthetic so decisively shapes our notions of language as members of the educated middle class, we might well ask if a reversal of this sequence could better accomplish our goals. Alternately, to the first and second stages of the inculcation of linguistic capital—that is, to the sequence of freshman writing and an introduction to literature—we might add a third. In this advanced writing course, students would study the relationships between popular ethos and aesthetic, a format that would arguably more adequately prepare them for the more specialized course work of their third and fourth years.

Similarly, we can reconsider the graduate curriculum's long-standing emphasis on research; clearly, if academic status and influence were to begin to rest more on teaching and service as well as on research and writing, then the distribution of courses in the PhD track also ought to reflect that shift. Here, too, ethnographic methodologies can help to ensure that future academics have a critical understanding of how English professors invest their own linguistic cultural capital in actual practice. Such courses, I believe, would counter the current cultural biases that have long overstated the efficacy of research writing and help to socialize the myriad modes of power actually exercised in universities. Here, too, a unionized and empowered faculty could explicitly discuss the sorts of skills necessary in the exercise of democratic self-government.

What's needed, finally, is an etiquette of popular ethos and formalist aesthetic, a pragmatics of usefulness and the ineffable, which would provide some guidance to students as well as to professors about the value of each. In Gerald Graff's terms, we can begin to teach the epistemological and professional conflicts that have shaped our departments as an explicit aspect of our courses and our professional programs. Traditionally, as PhDs in literature, English professionals who taught composition were certified as masters of the formalist aesthetic. Their mastery of the popular ethos was assumed, too often wrongly. Even today, as the number of advanced degrees in composition rises, few would argue that graduate programs in English studies should eliminate literature from their curricula. Composition PhDs, however, may well be doing just that. The logic of increasing specialization suggests that this may be only a temporary stage in the ongoing academic legitimization of composition. Yet I believe the research-based ideology traditional to literary studies risks denaturing our understanding of linguistic cultural capital. Indeed, in a political climate so fully dominated by vocational ideology and merit, this reliance may well prove our undoing. In seeking legitimacy through research writing, composition and rhetoric risk the nominal irrelevancy that has befallen literary studies. And, of course, a focus on disciplinary legitimating tends to minimize the need for new forms of institutional organization and power.

Guillory has argued that the current crisis of literary education illustrates that the cultural capital once offered by the New Criticism is no longer necessary to the economic game of postindustrial society and that it is "a form of capital increasingly marginal to the social function of the present education system" (x). Birnbaum reminds us that while we cannot ignore economics as such, it is not the only game in town. Life, as much as the study of English language and literature, is much more than a matter of employment and money. To succeed, too, we must develop our own rationale for the study of English language and literature, one "that will interest Congressmen and high school seniors" as well as parents and administrators (Birnbaum 19). In this sense, the survival of composition and literature is inexorably bound up in the struggle to maintain the relative autonomy of the university. In our own realm, we cannot succeed unless we are organized. In the larger public sphere, we have two main tasks. We must convince our audiences that an ethos of linguistic communication is a complex interaction of competencies and not a simple matter of grammatical fidelity. And we have to persuade them that a future without art is no future at all.

NOTES

WORKS CITED

INDEX

NOTES

1. My Father's Education

1. Perhaps surprisingly, but consistent with what I have called the silent or undocumented literacy of a man like my father, the city of Houston has no systematic archival process for the Department of Public Services or, indeed, for any other city agency. Consequently, I have been unable to confirm that the report that I found in my father's papers is identical in every respect to the official text he submitted to his superiors. Nevertheless, as this chapter seeks to demonstrate, it seems unlikely in the extreme that any of his official writing differed significantly from the popular ethos as I have defined it here. It is also important to remember that this sort of writing was in fact produced in collaboration with my father's secretary.

4. Ethos, Avocation, and the Liberal Arts

1. The increasing social and economic pressure on the middle class has been documented in a variety of contexts, from Jonathan Kozol's decades-long exploration of "desegregation" in the public schools to "Generation Broke," an investigation into student debt written by the Center for Responsible Lending's Tamara Draut and Javier Silva.

5. English Studies in an Age of Reform

1. In using the term "prophetic," I would like to acknowledge a debt to Cornel West's use of the term in *The American Evasion of Philosophy.*

WORKS CITED

Barrow, Clyde W. *Universities and the Capitalist State: Corporate Liberalism and the Reconstruction of the American Higher Education, 1894–1928.* History of American Thought and Culture ser., ed. Paul S. Boyer. Madison: U of Wisconsin P, 1990.

Berlin, James A. *Rhetoric and Reality: Writing Instruction in American Colleges, 1900–1985*. Carbondale: Southern Illinois UP, 1987.

———. *Writing Instruction in Nineteenth-Century American Colleges*. Carbondale: Southern Illinois UP, 1984.

Bhaskar, Roy. *Reclaiming Reality: A Critical Introduction to Contemporary Philosophy*. London: Verso, 1989.

Birnbaum, Robert. "Academic Leadership at the Millennium: Politics or Porcelain?" *Academe: The Bulletin of the American Association of University Professors* 85.3 (1999): 14–19.

Bloom, Lynn Z. "Freshman Composition as a Middle-Class Enterprise." *College English* 58.6 (1996): 654–75.

Bourdieu, Pierre. *Distinction: A Social Critique of the Judgment of Taste.* Trans. Richard Nice. Cambridge, Mass.: Harvard UP, 1984.

———. "The Forms of Capital." *Handbook of Theory and Research for the Sociology of Education*. Ed. John G. Richardson. New York: Greenwood, 1986. 241–58.

———. *Outline of a Theory of Practice*. Trans. Richard Nice. Cambridge: Cambridge UP, 1977.

Brandt, Deborah. "Accumulating Literacy." *College English* 57.6 (1995): 649-68.

———. "Writing for a Living: Literacy and the Knowledge Economy." *Written Communication* 22.2 (2005): 166–97.

Brooks, Cleanth. "Forty Years of Understanding Poetry." *CEA Journal* 10.4 (1980): 5–12.

———. *The Well Wrought Urn: Studies in the Structure of Poetry*. New York: Harvest, 1956.

———. "What Are English Teachers Teaching?" *NewsLetter of the College English Association* 2 (1940): 4. Republished in *CEA Critic* 33.1 (1970): 3–4.

Brooks, Cleanth, and Robert B. Heilman. *Understanding Drama*. New York: Holt, 1948.

Brooks, Cleanth, and Robert Penn Warren. *Modern Rhetoric*. New York: Harcourt, 1949.

———. *Understanding Poetry*. 3rd ed. New York: Holt, 1960.

Brooks, Cleanth, Robert Penn Warren, and John Thibaut Purser. *An Approach to Literature*. New York: Appleton, 1964.

Brown, John Seely. "Growing Up Digital: How the Web Changes Work, Education, and the Ways People Learn." *USDLA Journal* 16.2 (February 2002). October 9, 2008 <http://www.usdla.org/html/journal/FEB02_Issue/article01.html>.

Carton, Evan, and Gerald Graff. "Criticism since 1940." *The Cambridge History of American Literature*. Ed. Sacvan Bercovitch. Vol. 8. Cambridge: Cambridge UP, 1996. 263–388.

Crofts, Frederick S. *Textbooks Are Not Absolutely Dead Things*. Typophile Chap Book Series, ed. Frederick G. Melcher. New York: Grady, 1938.

Douglas, Wallace W. "Deliberate Exiles: The Social Sources of Agrarian Poetics." *Aspects of American Poetry*. Ed. Richard M. Ludwig. Columbus: Ohio State UP, 1962. 1273–1300.

Draut, Tamara, and Javier Silva. "Generation Broke: The Growth of Debt among Young People." *Demos*, October 1, 2004, 1–16. September 3, 2008 <http://www.demos-usa.org/home.cfm>.

Durst, Russell. *Collision Course: Conflict, Negotiation, and Learning in College Composition*. Urbana, Ill.: NCTE, 1999.

Eagleton, Terry. *Literary Theory: An Introduction*. Minneapolis: U of Minnesota P, 1983.

Ehrenreich, Barbara. *Fear of Falling: The Inner Life of the Middle Class*. New York: Pantheon, 1989.

Emerson, Ralph Waldo. "The American Scholar." *The Complete Works of Ralph Waldo Emerson*. Vol. 1, *Nature, Addresses and Lectures*. 1836, 1–12. *RWE.org*. October 9, 2008 <http://www.rwe.org/index.php?option=com_content&task=view&id=116&Itemid=42>.

Giroux, Henry A. *Ideology, Culture, and the Process of Schooling*. Philadelphia: Temple UP, 1981.

Godzich, Wlad. *The Culture of Literacy*. Cambridge, Mass.: Harvard UP, 1994.

Graff, Gerald. *Professing Literature: An Institutional History*. Chicago: U of Chicago P, 1987.

Guillory, John. *Cultural Capital: The Problem of Literary Canon Formation*. Chicago: U of Chicago P, 1993.

Hagge, John. "Early Engineering Textbooks and the Anthropological Complexity of Disciplinary Discourse." *Written Communication* 12.4 (October 1995): 439–91.

———. "The Spurious Paternity of Business Communication." *Journal of Business Communication* 26.1 (1989): 33–55.

Heath, Shirley Brice. *Ways with Words: Language, Life and Work in Communities and Classrooms*. Cambridge: Cambridge UP, 1983.

Hendricks, Bill. "Teaching Work: Academic Labor and Social Class." *JAC* 25.3 (2005): 586–622.

Hilgers, Thomas L., Edna Lardizabal Hussey, and Monica Stitt-Bergh. "As You're Writing, You Have These Epiphanies: What College Students Say about Writing and Learning in Their Majors." *Written Communication* 16.3 (1999): 317–53.

hooks, bell. *Teaching to Transgress: Education as the Practice of Freedom*. New York: Routledge, 1994.

Horner, Bruce. "Resisting Academics." *Insurrections: Approaches to Resistance in Composition Studies*. Ed. Andrea Greenbaum. Albany: State U of New York P, 2001. 169–84.

Hutchins, Edwin. *Cognition in the Wild*. Cambridge, Mass.: MIT P, 1995.

Kozol, Jonathan. *The Shame of the Nation: The Restoration of Apartheid Schooling in America*. New York: Three Rivers Press, 2005.

Latour, Bruno. *We Have Never Been Modern*. Trans. Catherine Porter. New York: Harvester Wheatsheaf, 1991.

Laurence, David. "MLA Survey of Staffing in English and Foreign Language Departments, Fall 1999." *Profession 2001*. New York: MLA, 2001. 211–24.

Lerner, Neal. "The Teacher-Student Writing Conference and the Desire for Intimacy." *College English* 68.2 (2005): 186–208.

Miller, Richard E. *As If Learning Mattered: Reforming Higher Education*. Ithaca: Cornell UP, 1998.

Miller, Susan. *Textual Carnivals: The Politics of Composition*. Carbondale: Southern Illinois UP, 1991.

Nora, Pierre. "Between Memory and History: Les Lieux de Memoire." Trans. Marc Roudebush. "Memory and Counter-Memory," special issue, *Representations* 26 (Spring 1989): 7–24.

North, Stephen M. *Refiguring the Ph.D. in English Studies: Writing, Doctoral Education, and the Fusion-Based Curriculum*. Urbana, Ill.: NCTE, 2000.

Ohmann, Richard. *English in America: A Radical View of the Profession*. New York: Oxford UP, 1976.

Palmer, Robert R., Bell I. Wiley, and William R. Keast. *The Army Ground Forces: The Procurement and Training of Ground Combat Troops*. Washington, D.C.: Office of the Chief of Military History, Department of the Army, 1948.

Parks, Stephen. *Class Politics: The Movement for the Students' Right to Their Own Language.* Urbana, Ill.: NCTE, 2000.

Radway, Janice A. *A Feeling for Books: The Book-of-the-Month Club, Literary Taste, and Middle-Class Desire.* Chapel Hill: U of North Carolina P, 1997.

Rodriguez, Richard. *Hunger of Memory: The Education of Richard Rodriguez.* Toronto: Bantam, 1982.

Rose, Mike. *Lives on the Boundary.* New York: Penguin, 1989.

Russell, David. *Writing in the Academic Disciplines, 1870–1990: A Curricular History.* Carbondale: Southern Illinois UP, 1991.

Sanders, Gerald D., Hoover H. Jordan, Robert M. Limpus, and Wallace H. Magoon. *Unified English Composition.* New York: Crofts, 1946.

Schroeder, Christopher. "Academic Literacies, Legitimacy Crises, and Electronic Cultures." *Journal of Literacy and Technology* 1.2 (Spring 2001). <http://www.literacyandtechnology.org/v1n2/schroeder/schrfrm.html>.

Seitz, James E. *Motives for Metaphor: Literacy, Curriculum Reform, and the Teaching of English.* Pittsburgh: U of Pittsburgh P, 1999.

Sheehan, Donald. *This Was Publishing: A Chronicle of the Book Trade in the Gilded Age.* Bloomington: Indiana UP, 1982.

Singer, Steve. "Man on Hot Seat: Phone Hike Reaction 'Bitter.'" *Houston Chronicle,* July 23, 1972, sec. 4, p. 1+.

Sledd, James. "Return to Service." *Composition Studies/Freshman English News* 28.2 (2000): 11–32.

Spurlin, William J., Michael Fisher, and Cleanth Brooks. "Afterword: An Interview with Cleanth Brooks." *New Criticism and Contemporary Literary Theory.* Ed. William J. Spurlin and Michael Fisher. New York: Garland, 1995. 365–83.

Watkins, Evan. *Work Time: English Departments and the Circulation of Cultural Value.* Stanford: Stanford UP, 1989.

Watkins, James Ray, Sr. "Rates and Research Major Activities 1972." Report, Rates and Research Division, Public Services Department, Houston, Tex., 1972.

West, Cornel. *The American Evasion of Philosophy: A Genealogy of Pragmatism.* Madison: U of Wisconsin P, 1989.

Wimsatt, W. K., and Monroe Beardsley. *The Verbal Icon: Studies in the Meaning of Poetry.* Lexington: U of Kentucky P, 1954.

Winchell, Mark Royden. *Cleanth Brooks and the Rise of Modern Criticism.* Charlottesville: UP of Virginia, 1996.

INDEX

James Ray Watkins Jr. has been a teacher for the last twenty years in a variety of places and levels. In the mid-1980s, he worked in the English as a Second Language program for the Peace Corps in the Philippines; in the late 1980s and early 1990s, he was an ESL tutor in Paris, France. For much of the 1990s, he taught freshman English in a computer classroom at the University of Texas at Austin, where he earned his PhD in 1999. Watkins also taught in a postdoctoral program at Temple University for a year and at Eastern Illinois University for six years. He now works exclusively online, teaching an occasional class for the Center for Talented Youth at Johns Hopkins University and serving as a full-time faculty member of the Art Institute of Pittsburgh Online. He has a Web site and blog at http://writinginthewild.com/.

OTHER BOOKS IN THE CCCC STUDIES IN WRITING & RHETORIC SERIES

African American Literacies Unleashed: Vernacular English and the Composition Classroom
Arnetha F. Ball and Ted Lardner

Rhetoric and Reality: Writing Instruction in American Colleges, 1900–1985
James A. Berlin

Writing Instruction in Nineteenth-Century American Colleges
James A. Berlin

Something Old, Something New: College Writing Teachers and Classroom Change
Wendy Bishop

The Variables of Composition: Process and Product in a Business Setting
Glenn J. Broadhead and Richard C. Freed

Audience Expectations and Teacher Demands
Robert Brooke and John Hendricks

Archives of Instruction: Nineteenth-Century Rhetorics, Readers, and Composition Books in the United States
Jean Ferguson Carr, Stephen L. Carr, and Lucille M. Schultz

Rehearsing New Roles: How College Students Develop as Writers
Lee Ann Carroll

Dialogue, Dialectic, and Conversation: A Social Perspective on the Function of Writing
Gregory Clark

Toward a Grammar of Passages
Richard M. Coe

A Communion of Friendship: Literacy, Spiritual Practice, and Women in Recovery
Beth Daniell

Rural Literacies
Kim Donehower, Charlotte Hogg, and Eileen E. Schell

Embodied Literacies: Imageword and a Poetics of Teaching
Kristie S. Fleckenstein

Writing with Authority: Students' Roles as Writers in Cross-National Perspective
David Foster

Writing Groups: History, Theory, and Implications
Anne Ruggles Gere

Sexuality and the Politics of Ethos in the Writing Classroom
Zan Meyer Gonçalves

Teaching/Writing in Thirdspaces: The Studio Approach
Rhonda C. Grego and Nancy S. Thompson

Computers & Composing: How the New Technologies Are Changing Writing
Jeanne W. Halpern and Sarah Liggett

Teaching Writing as a Second Language
Alice S. Horning

Revisionary Rhetoric, Feminist Pedagogy, and Multigenre Texts
Julie Jung

Women Writing the Academy: Audience, Authority, and Transformation
Gesa E. Kirsch

Invention as a Social Act
Karen Burke LeFevre

A New Perspective on Cohesion in Expository Paragraphs
Robin Bell Markels

Response to Reform: Composition and the Professionalization of Teaching
Margaret J. Marshall

Before Shaughnessy: Basic Writing at Yale and Harvard, 1920–1960
Kelly Ritter

Gender Influences: Reading Student Texts
Donnalee Rubin

The Young Composers: Composition's Beginnings in Nineteenth-Century Schools
Lucille M. Schultz

Multiliteracies for a Digital Age
Stuart A. Selber

Technology and Literacy in the Twenty-First Century: The Importance of Paying Attention
Cynthia L. Selfe

Language Diversity in the Classroom: From Intention to Practice
Edited by Geneva Smitherman and Victor Villanueva

Whistlin' and Crowin' Women of Appalachia: Literacy Practices since College
Katherine Kelleher Sohn

Across Property Lines: Textual Ownership in Writing Groups
Candace Spigelman

Personally Speaking: Experience as Evidence in Academic Discourse
Candace Spigelman

Self-Development and College Writing
Nick Tingle

Mutuality in the Rhetoric and Composition Classroom
David L. Wallace and Helen Rothschild Ewald

Evaluating College Writing Programs
Stephen P. Witte and Lester Faigley

Minor Re/Visions: Asian American Literacy Narratives as a Rhetoric of Citizenship
Morris Young